A Selected Bibliography of Significant Works About Adam Smith

A
Selected Bibliography
of Significant Works
About
ADAM SMITH

by *Martha Bolar Lightwood*

University of Pennsylvania Press
Philadelphia

Copyright © 1984 by the University of Pennsylvania Press

Library of Congress Cataloging in Publication Data

Lightwood, Martha Bolar.
  A selected bibliography of significant works about Adam Smith.

  Includes indexes.
    1. Smith, Adam, 1723–1790—Bibliography. I. Title.
Z8820.2.L53   1984   016.33015′3   84–3718
[HB103.S6]
ISBN 0–8122–7930–1

Printed in the United States of America

*To say anything new on Adam Smith is
not easy; but to say anything of
importance or profit, which has not
been said before, is well-nigh impossible.*

—LANGFORD L. PRICE

From a paper read before Section F of the
British Association at Edinburgh, 12 August
1892

Contents

Preface   ix

Introduction   xi

Bibliographic Works   1

Early Literature on Adam Smith   3

Biography   5

Influences on Adam Smith   6

Adam Smith's Influence on Economic, Social, and Philosophic
     Thought   7

General and Evaluative Studies   8

Methodology and the Nature of Inquiry   13

Historical and Literary Research   14

Smith's Place in the History of Political Economy   17

General Economic Theory   19

Price and Distribution Theory   22

Economic Growth and Development   24

International Economics   27

Profits and Interest   28

Monetary Theory and Policy   29

Labor Economics   30

Division of Labor   31

Public Finance   32

Free Markets and Regulation of the Economy   33

Technological Change   34

War and Defense   35

Philosophy and Moral Philosophy   36

Social Theory   40

Society and the Economy   42

Morality, Society, and the Individual   44

The Relationship of *Theory of Moral Sentiments* to *Wealth of Nations*   45

Government, Politics, and Law   46

The Colonies and the American Revolution   48

Miscellaneous Works   49

Collections of Readings   53

Brief Commentaries   54

Review Articles   57

Selected Editions of Smith's Works   58

The Glasgow Editions   59

Author Index   61

Title Index   67

Preface

This bibliography of significant articles and books published in English about Adam Smith between 1764 and 1982 is the result of a comprehensive literature search. All works selected for inclusion are listed in a form that will enable the reader to find them in library catalogs. Only published works are included; manuscript material except dissertations has been omitted.

While this compilation is not a *critical* bibliography, it is selective, in that I have omitted inconsequential works and those that would be of little interest to the contemporary reader. In the nineteenth century many commentaries on Adam Smith's works appeared within articles and books that were not written primarily on Adam Smith. In this book only a representative number of such contributions are included, since in my opinion most were rarely original and only infrequently contained insightful observations on Smith's work. My emphasis in this bibliography is on twentieth-century literature.

I wish to express my gratitude to Dr. Arthur I. Bloomfield, Professor of Economics at the University of Pennsylvania. He gave most generously of his time to furnish indispensable advice and constructive criticism, as well as answers to my many questions. Where this bibliography appears to have a coherent organization and a well-reasoned method of classification, it is owing to Dr. Bloomfield's guidance. Errors in categorization or in citation are mine, as are possible omissions of works which I may have failed to find. I am also grateful to the reference staff of the Van Pelt Library, University of Pennsylvania, from whom I received much assistance.

Introduction

In 1976 and for the preceding two years there was a considerable increase in the amount of distinguished literature on Adam Smith. This was the immediate result of interest aroused by the observance of the 200th anniversary of the first publication of Smith's most renowned work, *An Inquiry into the Nature and Causes of the Wealth of Nations*. However, an "Adam Smith renaissance" could be observed more than a decade earlier, especially within the discipline of economics. It was apparent that a new interest in the relationship between Smith's social and philosophic thought and his economic theory was emerging. The term "political economy" was reintroduced. Scholarly writers were becoming more concerned about the nature of the relationships among the state, the economic system, the needs of individuals, and the condition of society. Smith had dealt with these relationships.

Economists looked at Smith's contributions from an enlarged viewpoint, rediscovered the originality of much of his theory and analysis, and noted its relevance to contemporary problems. While Smith's works did not always hold ready solutions to questions of public policy, it was noted that he had been asking pertinent questions two centuries earlier. Matters that had not been of great interest at the time of the modest celebration of the centenary year of *The Wealth of Nations* now seemed significant. Certain doubts were raised about earlier views on Smith which had for many years been regarded as certitudes.

Complacency over traditional views of some of Smith's most significant work was shaken as his interest in the means of organization and control of society was seen to be closely tied to his concern with economic matters. Since then it has become increasingly apparent to a number of writers that an almost exclusive interest in *The Wealth of Nations* had caused the importance of his other works to be almost entirely overlooked. Too, the belief became more widespread that *The Wealth of Nations*, at least in the nineteenth and early twentieth centuries, had sometimes served as a convenient defense of much of what Smith had most severely criticized. Probably one reason the book enjoyed such enduring popularity, while it received little noneconomic evaluation, was the ease with which selected passages could be used to defend influential economic interests.

Many Smithian scholars now argue that Adam Smith did not consider capitalism an absolute good in itself, that instead it was the best way, in his judgment, by which personal freedom might be guaranteed and through which the economic growth he deemed so necessary to raise the income of the mass above the subsistence level could take place. To many economists and social theorists, it has become apparent that Smith's work in political economy was only one part of what Alec Macfie (1967) called "a general theory of society involving psychology and ethics, social and individual law, politics, and social philosophy."

There can be no doubt that Smith was in favor of the free market and of a limited government and that he recognized the primacy of self-interest as a motivating factor in human behavior. But it had not been frequently noticed that Smith was realist enough to recognize that self-interest is not always a material interest and that few people are invariably so rational as to recognize where their own interests might lie. What is now seen as a new and profoundly absorbing idea is the fact that Smith's work, when considered in its totality, represents a compelling interest in general social science, not solely economics.

A significant number of recent works on Smith included in this bibliography suggest that there is an increased awareness that Smith was arguing that his moral philosophy applied to the sphere of economic activity just as it did in personal relationships and social behavior. Self-interest was indeed dominant, but it was mediated by the process of sympathy and controlled by the mechanism of the impartial spectator, a complex and often ambiguous figure. The impression that Smith wrote in a very contemporary vein has grown as scholars became more aware that, in Smith's broad approach, the social and moral basis of the economic system was being continuously monitored and adjusted by the relationship between self-regard and sympathy and by the interaction of powerful noncoercive social controls with minimal but firmly enforced legal restraints.

Many present-day social theorists find themselves in agreement with Smith's assertion that man is above all a socialized being and strongly desires to act in accord with society's rules. This was much less obvious seventy-five years ago, or at least of less interest, and the literature of that period reflects this fact. Smith could, consistently, advocate a system that would grant extensive economic liberty to individuals and almost complete freedom from state interference with business enterprises because he was confident that the fear of social disapprobation would suppress the potential threat of such liberty. Government could be limited in its powers and thus be less dangerous because social pressures, since they are in accord with nature, are a stronger deterrent to greed and antisocial behavior in business than are state regulations. Both social and individual forces, and particularly the sympathy principle, combine to reduce conflict and to prevent the powerful self-interest motive from reaching a destructively high level.

Whether Smith's belief in the power of social rules to regulate economic activity was justified in his own lifetime seems impossible to verify or deny. Quite possibly it was not. The validity of the argument is perhaps even more in doubt today. In any event, the works contained in this bibliography suggest that there is now a tendency to reexamine Smith's social and philosophical views as well as his economic theory. This tendency must be considered a promising one. Even though it cannot be shown that Smith created a comprehensive theory either of society or of economics, he did succeed remarkably well in connecting isolated pieces of knowledge and partial explanations, and he demonstrated relationships among phenomena that had not previously been seen as connected.

Further serious consideration of all the works of Adam Smith will be a worthy and productive effort. The nature of much Smithian literature shows that such work has already begun. We may be certain that no one will ever produce a "correct" interpretation of Smith's work. Those who share my admiration for him will also agree with Edmund Burke, who wrote to Smith these words of praise:

> *"A theory like yours, founded on the nature of man, which is always the same, will last, when those that are founded on his opinions, which are always changing, will and must be forgotten."*

THE LITERATURE SEARCH

The search for relevant literature to make a part of this bibliography included examining all volumes and supplements to appropriate indexes and abstracting services; printed catalogs of books, with their supplements; book-form bibliographies; and citations in footnotes and bibliographies appended to selected articles and books about Adam Smith.

The indexes and abstracts consulted were the following: *ABC Political Science; Advance Bibliography of Contents: Political Science and Government; Business Periodicals Index* (Wilson); *Bulletin Signaletique Philosophie, Sociologie, Ethnologie* (Centre de Documentation du C.N.R.S.); *Essay and General Literature Index* (Wilson); *Historical Abstracts* (American Bibliographic Center); *Index of Economic Articles* (American Economic Association); *International Bibliography of Economics* (UNESCO); *Journal of Economic Literature* (American Economic Association); *New York Times Index* (New York Times); *Nineteenth Century Readers' Guide to Periodical Literature, 1890–1922* (Wilson); *Philosopher's Index* (Bowling Green University); *Poole's Index to Periodical Literature, 1801–1881,* and supplements (Houghton); *Public Affairs Information Service* (Public Affairs Information Service); *Readers' Guide to Periodical Literature* (Wilson); *Social Science Abstracts* (Columbia University); *Social Science Citation Index* (Institute for Scientific Information); *Social Science Index* (Wilson); *Wall Street Journal Index* (Wall Street Journal).

The following are extensive listings of books, such as national bibliographies, which were of value in the search. *Author-Title Catalog of the Baker Library, Graduate School of Business Administration, Harvard University. Supplements. Subject Catalog* (G. K. Hall); *British National Bibliography,* and subject catalog (British Museum); *Cumulative Book Index,* and supplements (Wilson); *Dictionary Catalog of the Research Libraries of the New York Public Library* (New York Public Library); *Dissertation Abstracts* (University Microfilms International); *Forthcoming Books* (Bowker); *General Catalogue of Printed Books* (British Museum); *National Union Catalog* (Library of Congress); *United States Catalog. Books in Print, 1928* (Wilson); *Wellesley Index to Victorian Periodicals* (Routledge & Paul).

The tables of contents of all volumes of certain journals that frequently publish contributions about Adam Smith were examined. This search revealed literature that had not been included in indexes. Those journals were: *History of Political Economy; Scottish Journal of Political Economy; Journal of the History of Ideas; Review of Economic Studies; Oxford Economic Papers; Journal of Economic Issues; Quarterly Journal of Economics; Journal of Philosophic Studies; Economic Journal; Economic Record;* and *American Economic Review.*

ORGANIZATION AND CITATION OF REFERENCES

Contents of the body of this work consist of thirty-four major categories. The decision to have a large number of categories was based on the desire to classify references as narrowly as possible since there were to be no abstracts of references. Under each category, journal articles appear first, followed by books and parts of books.

Certain categories require explanation. "Early Literature on Adam Smith" has no specific cutoff date but in general includes works written before the importance of Smith's future place in the history of economic theory and philosophy had been recognized. "General and Evaulative Studies" consists of works about Smith which, while of significant interest, are not unique and do not contain new insights into his writings or original interpretations of them. "International Economics" includes the topics of international trade and international finance. "Division of Labor" is shown separately from "Labor Economics" since this aspect of Smith's work has received an unusual amount of commentary because it reveals his insight into a contemporary problem and combines the idea of economic growth with its concomitant effects on human behavior and the condition of society.

"Brief Commentaries" should not be regarded as a comprehensive listing of short observations on the work of Adam Smith. Completeness here would require listing almost every book on the history of economics. I have attempted to be selective within this category. "Selected Editions of Smith's Works" contains citations of a few significant editions of Smith's works, arranged in alphabetical order by title. Various editions of each title are arranged by the date of publication of the edition cited. No attempt has been made to cite all editions of any title. A comprehensive listing may be found in *The Vanderblue Memorial Collection of Smithiana . . . and a Catalogue of the Collection,* cited in this book under "Bibliographic Works." The editions commissioned by the University of Glasgow to celebrate the 200th anniversary of the first publication of *The Wealth of Nations* are in the "Glasgow Editions" category.

I have not included general reference sources that could be used to identify literature about Smith. The reader is referred to the section of the Introduction entitled "The Literature Search." Further use of the publications listed there should make it possible to add literature citations to this compilation in the future.

I was able to examine almost all the works cited in this book. Where I could not find some of them, the references were categorized on the basis of annotations in other works or by the context in which I had located the references. The form of the citations is bibliographically correct. They are arranged, in the body of the work, by the approved Library of Congress "main entry," whether a personal name or a corporate body. Where it was not possible, after considerable research, to identify an author's first name, some authors' names are shown with an initial in lieu of a first name. When the month of issue of a journal article could not be determined, inclusive pagination, and the number of the issue if that is known, is given. Where a chapter or section of a titled contribution to a collection is a distinct part of a book, the pagination of that portion of the book has been shown. Where unique or important comments on Adam Smith were not placed within a single section of a book, groups of page numbers are not given. Some references are followed by a short, descriptive comment in parentheses as an explanation. These are not annotations.

This bibliography has two indexes: the first is an alphabetic index to the names of authors of works cited; the second is an index to the titles of works cited. In all parts of the book I have used a letter-by-letter method of alphabetizing, punctuation being disregarded. Certain agreed-on exceptions, made to help the reader, were followed in all cases. (Example: last names of authors beginning with "M'," "Mc," and "Mac" are alphabetized *as though* they were all spelled "Mac——.")

Each citation appears only once in this book, except when a title has been published one or more times as a journal article and again as a reading in a collection. Similarly, an identical title may appear twice if it is the title of a doctoral dissertation and also published as a book under the same title.

The numbering system used in the indexes refers to the item numbers which appear in sequential order to the left of each citation in the body of the book.

Bibliographic Works

ARTICLES

001 Bonar, James. [Addenda to] "A Catalogue of the Library of Adam Smith." *Economic Journal* 44 (June 1934): 349.

002 Bonar, James. [Addenda to] "A Catalogue of the Library of Adam Smith." *Economic Journal* 46 (March 1936): 178.

003 Bordo, M. D., and Landau, D. "The Pattern of Citations in Economic Theory, 1945–68: An Exploration Towards a Quantitative History of Thought." *History of Political Economy* 11 (Summer 1979): 240–53.

004 Jones, Claude. "Adam Smith's Library—Some Additions by Claude Jones [to Bonar's Catalogue]" *Economic History* 4 (February 1940): 326–28.

005 MacGarvey, C. J. "Notes on Adam Smith's Library and the Bonar Catalogue, 1932." *Economic Journal* 59 (June 1949): 259–64.

006 Rechtenwald, Horst C. "An Adam Smith Renaissance *anno* 1976? The Bicentenary Output—A Reappraisal of His Scholarship." *Journal of Economic Literature* 16 (March 1978): 56–83.

007 West, Edwin G. "Scotland's Resurgent Economist: A Survey of the New Literature on Adam Smith." *Southern Economic Journal* 45 (October 1978): 343–69.

BOOKS

008 Amano, Keitaro. "Part 1. Adam Smith." In his *Bibliography of the Classical Economics*, pp. 31–130. Science Council of Japan, Division of Economics, Commerce, and Business Administration, Economic Series, no. 27. Tokyo: Science Council of Japan, 1961.

009 Bonar, James. *A Catalogue of the Library of Adam Smith, Author of the "Moral Sentiments" and the "Wealth of Nations."* London: Macmillian Co., 1894.

010   Bonar, James. *A Catalogue of the Library of Adam Smith, Author of the "Moral Sentiments" and "The Wealth of Nations."* 2d ed. London: Macmillian Co., 1932

011   Bowman, Richard. *A Bibliographic List of Essays on the Economic Theory of Adam Smith.* Los Angeles: Universal Publishing Co., 1941.

012   Carpenter, Kenneth E. *Dialogue in Political Economy: Translations from and into German in the 18th Century.* Kress Library Publication, no. 23. Boston: Baker Library, Harvard University Graduate School of Business Administration, 1977.

013   Franklin, Burt, and Cordasco, Francesco. *Adam Smith, a Bibliographical Checklist: An International Record of Critical Writings and Scholarship Relating to Smith and Smithian Theory, 1876–1950.* New York: B. Franklin, 1950.

014   Harvard University. Graduate School of Business Administration. Baker Library. *The Vanderblue Memorial Collection of Smithiana, An Essay by J. Charles Bullock, and a Catalogue of the Collection Presented to the Harvard Business School by Homer B. Vanderblue* . . . . Kress Library of Business and Economics Publication, no. 2. Boston: Baker Library, Harvard Graduate School of Business Administration, 1939.

015   Mizuti, Hiroshi. *Adam Smith's Library: A Supplement to Bonar's Catalogue, with a Checklist of the Whole Library.* Cambridge: Cambridge University Press, 1967.

016   Murray, David. *French Translations of the Wealth of the Nations.* Glasgow: MacLehose, 1905.

017   Scott, William R. "Studies Relating to Adam Smith During the Last Fifty Years." In *Proceedings of the British Academy*, vol. 26, 1940, edited by Alec L. Macfie, pp. 249–74. London: The Academy. Reprinted, London: Milford, 1941; Clarendon: Oxford University Press, 1941.

018   Sturges, R. P., comp. *Economists' Papers 1750–1950: A Guide to Archive and Other Manuscript Sources for the History of British and Irish Economic Thought.* Durham, N.C.: Duke University Press, 1975.

019   Vanderblue, Homer B. *Adam Smith and the "Wealth of Nations": An Adventure in Book Collecting and a Bibliography.* Boston: Baker Library, Harvard Graduate School of Business Administration, 1936.

020   Yanaihara, Tadao. *A Full and Detailed Catalogue of Books Which Belonged to Adam Smith, Now in the Possession of the Faculty of*

Economics, University of Tokyo, with Notes and Explanations.
Tokyo: Iwanami Shoten, 1951.

Early Literature on Adam Smith

ARTICLES

021 "The 'Wealth of the Nations,' with Notes, Supplementary Chapters,
and a Life of Dr. Smith." *Edinburgh Review* 7 (January 1806):
470–71. (Review of a book by William Playfair, London, 1805.)

BOOKS

022 [Archard, T.] *Suppression of the French Nobility Vindicated, in an
Essay on Their Origin and Qualities, Moral and Intellectual, by
the Rev. T. A. * * * a Paris; To Which Is Added a Comparative
View of Dr. Smith's System of the Wealth of Nations with Regard
to France and England.* London: Debrett, 1792.

023 Bentham, Jeremy. *Defence of Usury, Shewing the Impolicy of the
Present Legal Restraints on the Terms of Pecuniary Bargains, in a
Series of Letters to a Friend, to Which Is Added a Letter to Adam
Smith . . . on the Discouragements Opposed by the Above Re-
straints to the Progress of Inventive Industry . . . .* 2d ed. London:
T. Payne, 1790.

024 Buchanan, David. *Observations on the Subjects Treated in Dr. Smith's
"Inquiry into the Nature and Cause [sic] of the Wealth of Nations."*
London: Ogles, Duncan, and Cochran, 1817.

025 Burton, John H. *Life and Correspondence of David Hume. Contains
Numerous Letters from David Hume to Adam Smith, Together
with an Account of their Friendship.* 2 vols. Edinburgh: W. Tait,
1816.

026 [Carlyle, Alexander.] *A Letter to His Grace the Duke of Buccleugh on
National Defence, with Some Remarks on Dr. Smith's Chapter on
the Subject in His Book Entitled "An Inquiry into the Nature and
Causes of Wealth of Nations,"* by M. T. London, 1778.

027 [Gray, John.] *The Essential Principles of the Wealth of Nations, Illus-*

trated, in Opposition to Some False Doctrines of Dr. Adam Smith and Others. London: Becket, 1797.

028 [Gray, Simon.] *All Classes Productive of National Wealth; Or, The Theories of M. Quesnai, Dr. Adam Smith and Mr. Gray Concerning the Various Classes of Men as to the Production of Wealth to the Community Analyzed and Examined,* by George Purves [Simon Gray]. London: Longmans, 1817.

029 [Horne, George, Bishop of Norwich.] *A Letter to Adam Smith LL.D. on the Life, Death, and Philosophy of His Friend David Hume Esq., by One of the People called Christians.* . . . 2d ed. Oxford: Clarendon Press, 1777.

030 Hume, David. *The Life of David Hume, Esq., Written by Himself.* London: W. Strahan & T. Cadell, 1777. (Includes a letter from Adam Smith to William Strahan.)

031 [Joerson, S. A.] *Adam Smith, Author of "An Inquiry into the Nature and Causes of the Wealth of Nations," and Thomas Paine, Author of "The Decline and Fall of the English System of Finance.* . . ." Hamburg: Perthes, 1796.

032 Joyce, Jeremiah. *A Complete Analysis or Abridgement of Dr. Adam Smith's "Inquiry into the Nature and Causes of the Wealth of Nations."* Cambridge: J. Deighton, 1797.

033 Law, James T., Chancellor of Lichfield. *The Poor Man's Garden; Or, a Few Brief Rules for Regulating Allotments of Land to the Poor, for Potatoe Gardens, with a Reference to the Opinions of Dr. A. Smith in His "Wealth of Nations."* London, 1830.

034 [Lee, Arthur.] *An Essay in Vindication of the Continental Colonies of America, from a Censure of Mr. Adam Smith, in His Theory of Moral Sentiments, With Some Reflections on Slavery in General,* by An American. London: Arthur Lee, 1764.

035 Pownall, Thomas. *A Letter from Governor Pownall to Adam Smith . . . Being an Examination of Several Points of Doctrine, Laid Down in His "Inquiry into the Nature and Causes of The Wealth of Nations."* London: J. Almon, 1776.

036 Smith, Adam. *Letter from Adam Smith, LL.D., to Mr. Strahan [upon] the Death of Hume.* London: W. Strahan & T. Cadell, 1777.

037 Smith, Adam. *A Letter to Sir William Pultney, in Consequence of His Proposal for Establishing a New Bank.* London, 1797. (Appears in vol. 231, *College Pamphlets.*)

038 West, Edward. *Price of Corn and Wages of Labour, with Observations upon Dr. Smith's and Mr. Ricardo's Doctrines upon Those Subjects* . . . . London, 1826.

039 Young, William. *Corn Trade, an Examination of Certain Commercial Principles, in Their Application to Agriculture and the Corn Trade, as Laid Down in the Fourth Book of Mr. Adam Smith's Treatise on the "Wealth of Nations," with Proposals for Revival of the Statutes Against Forestalling.* . . . New ed. London: J. Stockdale, 1800.

Biography

ARTICLES

040 Bell, John F. "Adam Smith, Clubman." *Scottish Journal of Political Economy* 7 (June 1960): 108–16.

041 Clark, Andrew. "Adam Smith's Status at Oxford." *Notes and Queries*, 10th ser., 12 (1909): 384.

042 Elliott, A. R. D. "Adam Smith and His Friends." *Edinburgh Review* 182 (July 1895): 221–48.

043 Robertson, E. S. "The Author of the *Wealth of Nations*." *Dublin University Magazine* 42 (1878): 452–68.

044 Bagehot, Walter. "Adam Smith as a Person." In his *Bagehot's Historical Essays*, edited and with an introduction by Norman St. John-Stevas, pp. 79–146. Garden City, N.Y.: Anchor Books, 1965. (First published in *Fortnightly Review*, 1876.)

045 [Draper, William.] *Life of Dr. Adam Smith*. London: Baldwin & Cradock, 1833. (Extract from *Lives of Eminent Persons*, London, 1833.)

046 Fay, Charles R. *Adam Smith, and the Scotland of His Day*. Publications of the Department of Social and Economic Research, University of Glasgow, no. 3. Cambridge: Cambridge University Press, 1956.

047 Fulton, R. B. *Adam Smith Speaks to Our Times: A Study of His Ethical Ideas*. Boston: Christopher, 1963.

048 Haldane, Richard B. *The Life of Adam Smith*. London: Scott, 1887.

049 Hirst, Francis W. *Adam Smith*. New York: Macmillan & Co., 1904. Reprint ed., Folcroft, Pa.: Folcroft, 1977.

050 Kay, John. *A Series of Original Portraits and Caricature Etchings . . . with Biographical Sketches and Illustrative Anecdotes*. 2 vols. Edinburgh: A. & C. Black, 1877. (Contains portraits of Adam Smith opposite pp. 72 and 75.)

051 McCulloch, John R. [Introduction to] *"An Inquiry into the Nature and Causes of the Wealth of the Nations," by Adam Smith*. "A Life of the Author, an Introductory Discourse, Notes, and Supplemental Dissertations." 4 vols. Edinburgh: A. Black & W. Tait, 1828.

052 McCulloch, John R. *Sketch of the Life and Writings of Adam Smith, LL.D*. Edinburgh: Murray & Gibb, 1855.

053 McCulloch, John R. "Sketch of the Life and Writings of Adam Smith." In his *Treatises and Essays on Subjects Connected with Economical Policy: With Biographical Sketches on Quesnay, Adam Smith, and Ricardo*. Edinburgh: Black, 1853.

054 Mossner, Ernest C. *Adam Smith: The Biographical Approach*. David Murray Lectures 30. Glasgow University Publication 134. Glasgow: University of Glasgow Press, 1969.

055 Rae, John. *Life of Adam Smith*. New York: Macmillan Co., 1895. Reprint ed., New York: Kelley, 1965.

056 Scott, William R. *Adam Smith as Student and Professor, with Unpublished Documents, Including Parts of the "Edinburgh Lectures," a Draft of "The Wealth of Nations," Extracts from the Muniments of the University of Glasgow and Correspondence*. Glasgow University Publications 46. Glasgow: Jackson, 1937.

057 Stewart, Dugald. *Biographical Memoir of Adam Smith, LL.D., of William Robertson, D.D., and Thomas Reid, D.D*. Read before the Royal Society of Edinburgh. Edinburgh: G. Ramsay, 1811.

058 Viner, Jacob. "Guide to John Rae's Life of Adam Smith." In *Life of Adam Smith*, by John Rae, pp. 1–36. Reprint ed., New York: Kelley, 1965.

Influences on Adam Smith

BOOKS

059 Chamley, P. E. "The Conflict Between Montesquieu and Hume: A Study of the Origins of Adam Smith's Universalism." In *Essays on Adam Smith*, edited by Andrew S. Skinner and Thomas Wilson, pp. 274–305. Oxford: Clarendon Press, 1975.

060 Merkel, Edward T. "Henry Home of Kames as Predecessor to Adam Smith." Ph.D. dissertation, Northern Illinois University, 1974.

061 Raphael, David D. " 'The True Old Humean Philosophy' and Its Influ-

ence on Adam Smith." In *David Hume: Bicentenary Papers*, edited by G. P. Morice, pp. 23–38. Austin, Tex.: University of Texas at Austin Press, 1977.

062 Scott, William R. *Francis Hutcheson: His Life, Teaching, and Position in the History of Philosophy.* Cambridge: Cambridge University Press, 1900. Reprint ed., New York: Kelley, 1966.

063 Scott, William R. *Greek Influence on Adam Smith.* Athens: Pyrsos Press, 1939.

064 Taylor, William L. *Francis Hutcheson and David Hume as Predecessors of Adam Smith.* Durham, N.C.: Duke University Press, 1965.

Adam Smith's Influence on Economic, Social, and Philosophic Thought

ARTICLES

065 Coase, Ronald H. "The *Wealth of Nations.*" *Economic Inquiry* 15 (July 1977): 309–25.

066 Dickinson, H. T. "The Politics of Edward Gibbon." *Literature and History* 8 (1978): 175–96.

067 Gottfried, P. "Adam Smith and German Social Thought." *Modern Age* 21 (Spring 1977): 146–52.

068 Henderson, John P. "Adam Smith, Ricardo, and Economic Theory." *Centennial Review* 21, no. 2 (1977): 118–39.

069 Johnson, Harry G. "The Relevance of *The Wealth of Nations* to Contemporary Economic Policy." *Scottish Journal of Political Economy* 23, no. 2 (1976): 171–76.

070 Price, Langford L. "Adam Smith and His Relations to Recent Economics." *Economic Journal* 3 (June 1893): 239–54.

071 Schweber, Silvan S. "Darwin and the Political Economists: Divergence of Character." *Journal of the History of Biology* 13, no. 2 (1980): 195–289.

072 Schweber, Silvan S. "The Origin of the Origin Revisited." *Journal of the History of Biology* 10, no. 2 (1977): 229–316.

073 Skinner, Andrew S. "Adam Smith: An Aspect of Modern Economics?" *Scottish Journal of Political Economy* 26 (June 1979): 109–25.

074 Taylor, N. W. "Adam Smith's First Russian Disciple." *Slavonic and East European Review* 45 (July 1967): 425–38.

075 Wykes, Alan. "Pitt as Chancellor of the Exchequer." *British History Illustrated* 2, no. 2 (1975): 2–11.

BOOKS

076 Bronowski, Jacob, and Mazlish, Bruce. "Adam Smith." In their *The Western Intellectual Tradition*, pp. 336–56. New York: Harper & Row, 1960.

077 Brown, A. H. "Adam Smith's First Russian Followers." In *Essays on Adam Smith*, edited by Andrew S. Skinner and Thomas Wilson, pp. 247–73. Oxford: Clarendon Press, 1975.

078 Brown, A. H., and Desnitsky, S. E. "Adam Smith and the Nakaz of Catherine II." In *Oxford Slavonic Papers*, edited by Robert Auty, J. L. I. Fennell, and I. P. Foote, new series, vol. 7, pp. 42–59. Oxford University Press, 1974– .

079 Hetzel, Robert L. *The Relevance of Adam Smith*. Richmond, Va.: Federal Reserve Bank of Richmond, 1977.

080 Hollander, Jacob H. "The Dawn of a Science." In *Adam Smith, 1776–1926 . . .* , by John M. Clark et al., pp. 22–52. Chicago: University of Chicago Press, 1928. Reprint ed., New York: Kelley, 1966.

081 Hollander, Jacob H. "The Founder of a School." In *Adam Smith, 1776–1926 . . .* , by John M. Clark et al., pp. 1–21. Chicago: University of Chicago Press, 1928. Reprint ed., New York: Kelley, 1966.

082 Lowe, Robert. "What Are the More Important Results Which Have Followed from the Publication of the *Wealth of Nations . . .* ?" Address [before the Political Economy Club, London, 1881]. London: The Club, 1876.

083 Price, Langford L. "Adam Smith and His Relation to Recent Economics." In his *Economic Science and Practice*, chap. 12. London: Methuen, 1896.

084 Rima, Ingrid H. *Development of Economic Analysis*. 3d ed. Homewood, Ill.: Irwin, 1972.

General and Evaluative Studies

ARTICLES

085 Bagehot, Walter. "Adam Smith as a Person." *Fortnightly Review*, n.s., 26 (July 1876): 18–42.

086 Bonar, James. "Adam Smith, 1723 and 1923." *Economica* 3 (June 1923): 89–92.

087 Boulding, Kenneth E. "After Samuelson, Who Needs Adam Smith?" *History of Political Economy* 3 (Fall 1971): 225–37.

088 Cannan, Edwin. "Adam Smith as an Economist." *Economica* 6 (June 1926): 123–34.

089 Dankert, Clyde E. "On the *Wealth of Nations.*" *South Atlantic Quarterly* 66 (Spring 1967): 245–55.

090 Elliott, John E. "The Political Economy of Adam Smith: Then and Now." *National Forum* 58 (Summer 1978): 41–45.

091 Fay, Charles R. "Adam Smith and the Dynamic State." *Economic Journal* 40 (March 1930): 25–34.

092 Franklin, Raymond S. "Smithian Economics and Its Pernicious Legacy." *Review of Social Economy* 34 (December 1976): 379–89.

093 Golden, Soma. "Adam Smith's Economics Revived in Election Year." *New York Times,* March 9, 1976, 35 +.

094 Gray, Alexander. "Adam Smith." *Scottish Journal of Political Economy* 23 (June 1976): 153–69.

095 Heilbroner, Robert L. "Homage to Adam Smith." *Challenge* 19 (March-April 1976): 6–11.

096 Hollander, Jacob H. "Adam Smith, 1776–1926." *Journal of Political Economy* 35 (April 1927): 153–97. (Lectures given at the University of California, December 9 and 10, 1926.)

097 Hollander, Samuel. "Smith and Ricardo: Aspects of the Nineteenth-century Legacy." *American Economic Review* 67 (February 1977): 37–41.

098 Hutchison, Terrance W. "Adam Smith and the *Wealth of Nations.*" *Journal of Law and Economics* 19 (October 1976): 507–28.

099 Jaffé, William. "A Centenarian on a Bicentenarian: Leon Walras's *Elements* of Adam Smith's *Wealth of Nations.*" *Canadian Journal of Economics* 10 (February 1977): 19–33.

100 Jensen, Hans E. "Sources and Contours of Adam Smith's Conceptualized Reality in the *Wealth of Nations.*" *Review of Social Economy* 34 (December 1976): 259–74.

101 Leacock, Stephen. "What Is Left of Adam Smith?" *Canadian Journal of Economics and Political Science* 1 (February 1935): 41–51.

102 Leslie, Thomas Edward Cliffe. "The Political Economy of Adam Smith." *Fortnightly Review,* n.s., 14 (November 1870): 549–63.

103 Letwin, W. "Adam Smith: Re-reading the Wealth of Nations." *Encounter* 46 (March 1976): 45–53.

104 Mann, Fritz K. "Adam Smith—The Heir and the Ancestor." *Zeit-*

schrift für die Gestamte Staatwissenschaft 132 (October 1976): 683–90.

105 [Marriott, J. A. R.] "Adam Smith and Some Problems of Today." *Fortnightly Review*, n.s., 76 (December 1904): 969–81.

106 Moss, Laurence S. "The Economics of Adam Smith: Professor Hollander's Reappraisal." *History of Political Economy* 8 (Winter 1976): 564–74.

107 Murchison, Claudius. "Revising Adam Smith." *Virginia Quarterly Review* 11 (1935): 496–505.

108 Parish, William J. "With Due Respect to Adam Smith." *Southwestern Social Science Quarterly* 26 (December 1945): 217–27.

109 Paul, Ellen F. "Adam Smith: A Reappraisal." *Journal of Libertarian Studies* 1 (Fall 1977): 289–306.

110 Plenty, Arthur J. "Jettisoning of Adam Smith." *American Review* 4 (January 1935): 326–36.

111 Roll, Eric. "*The Wealth of Nations*, 1776–1976." *Lloyds Bank Review* 119 (January 1976): 12–22.

112 Samuels, Warren J. "The Political Economy of Adam Smith." *Ethics* 87 (April 1977): 189–207.

113 Samuels, Warren J. "The Political Economy of Adam Smith." *Nebraska Journal of Economics and Business* 15 (Summer 1976): 3–24.

114 Stigler, George J. "The Successes and Failures of Professor Smith." *Journal of Political Economy* 84 (December 1976): 1199–1213.

115 Viner, Jacob. "Adam Smith and Laissez-faire." *Journal of Political Economy* 35 (April 1927): 198–232.

BOOKS

116 *The Adam Smith Centennial [to Commemorate the Hundredth Anniversary of the Publication of the "Wealth of Nations"]*. New York, 1876. (First appeared in issue no. 10 of *New Century*, 1876.)

117 Angus-Butterworth, Lionel M. "Adam Smith." In his *Ten Master Historians*, pp. 23–38. Aberdeen: Aberdeen University Press, 1962.

118 Anikin, Andreï V. *A Science in Its Youth: Pre-Marxian Political Economy*. Translated by K. M. Cook. New York: International Publishers, 1979.

119 Bagehot, Walter. "Adam Smith and Our Modern Economy." In his *Economic Studies*, pp. 125–75. London: Longmans, Green, 1888.

120   Black, R. D. Collison, ed. *Readings in the Development of Economic Analysis 1776–1848*. New York: Barnes & Noble, 1971.

121   Bonar, James. "Adam Smith." In his *Philosophy and Political Economy in Some of Their Historical Relations*, pp. 146–83. London: Allen & Unwin, 1893. Reprint ed., New York: Humanities Press, 1968.

122   Campbell, Roy H. *Adam Smith*, by R. H. Campbell and A. S. Skinner. New York: St. Martin's, 1982.

123   Campbell, T. D., and Ross, Ian C. "The Theory of the Wise and Virtuous Man: Reflections on Adam Smith's Response to Hume's Deathbed Wish." In *Studies in Eighteenth Century Culture*, edited by Harry C. Payne, pp. 65–74. Madison, Wis.: University of Wisconsin Press, 1982.

124   Dankert, Clyde E. *Adam Smith: Man of Letters and Economist*. Hicksville, N.Y.: Exposition Press, 1974.

125   Ekelund, R. B. "Adam Smith (1723–1790)." In his *A History of Economic Theory and Method*, pp. 57–75. New York: McGraw-Hill, 1975.

126   *Encyclopedia of the Social Sciences*. S. v. "Smith, Adam (1723–90)," by John M. Clark.

127   Fanfani, Amitori. *Adam Smith's Doctrine and the Present-day Crisis*. Rome: Azinende Tipographiche Eridi G. Bardi, 1977(?). (Text of a lecture given by Professor Amitori Fanfani at the University of Keio, Tokyo, on April 8, 1977.)

128   Galbraith, John K. "The Founding Faith: Adam Smith's *Wealth of Nations*." In his *Annals of an Abiding Liberal*, edited by Andrea D. Williams, pp. 86–102. Boston: Houghton Mifflin, 1979.

129   Gide, Charles, and Rist, Charles. "Adam Smith." In *History of Economic Doctrines from the Time of the Physiocrats to the Present Day*, pp. 68–133. Authorized translation from the 2d rev. and augmented ed. of 1913. London: Harrop, 1943.

130   Ginsberg, Eli. *The House of Adam Smith*. New York: Columbia University Press, 1934.

131   Ginsberg, Eli. "The House of Adam Smith." Ph.D. dissertation, Columbia University, 1935.

132   Graham, Malcolm K. *The Synthetic "Wealth of Nations": An Inquiry into . . ."Wealth of Nations," by Adam Smith, LL.D.*, condensed and extended by Malcolm K. Graham. Nashville, Tenn.: Parthenon, 1937.

133   Haggarty, John, ed. *The Wisdom of Adam Smith*. Edited with an introduction by Benjamin A. Rogge. Indianapolis: Liberty

Fund, 1976. (Short observations by Smith on twenty-four subjects.)

134 Hirschman, Albert O. "Adam Smith and the End of a Vision." In his *The Passions and the Interests: Political Arguments for Capitalism Before Its Triumph*, pp. 100–113. Princeton: Princeton University Press, 1977.

135 *International Encyclopedia of the Social Sciences*. S.v. "Smith, Adam," by Jacob Viner.

136 Lerner, Max. "The Paradox of Adam Smith." In his *Ideas Are Weapons: The History and Uses of Ideas*, pp. 297–304. New York: Viking, 1939.

137 MacPherson, Hector C. *Adam Smith*. Edinburgh: Oliphant, 1899.

138 Mitchell, Wesley C. "Adam Smith." In his *Lecture Notes on Types of Economic Theory*, vol. 1, pp. 8–81. New York: Kelley, 1949.

139 Nicholson, Joseph S. *Introductory Essay on Adam Smith's "Wealth of Nations . . . "*. [Edinburgh], 1883.

140 Oser, Jacob. "The Classical School: Adam Smith." In his *The Evolution of Economic Thought*, 2d ed., pp. 55–77. New York: Harcourt, Brace, 1970.

141 Pike, Edgar R. *Adam Smith: Father of the Science of Economics*. New York: Hawthorne Books, 1965.

142 Putnam, Oliver. "Observations on Smith's *Wealth of Nations*." In his *Tracts of Sundry Topics of Political Economy*, chap. 2. Boston: Russell, Odiorne, 1930. Reprint ed., New York: Kelley, 1970.

143 Robertson, Hector M. *The Adam Smith Tradition: Inaugural Lectures Delivered Before the University of Cape Town on 13 October 1950*. Cape Town, South Africa: Oxford University Press, 1950.

144 Roll, Erich. "Adam Smith." In his *A History of Economic Thought*, 3d ed., pp. 142–73. London: Faber, 1956.

145 Scott, William R. *Adam Smith: An Oration*. Glasgow University Publications 48. Glasgow: Jackson, 1938. (Delivered at the University on Commencement Day, June 22, 1938.)

146 Stewart, Dugald, "An Account of the Life and Writings of Adam Smith." In *The Works of Dugald Stewart*, edited by Sir William B. Hamilton. Edinburgh: Constable, 1858. (From *Transactions of the Royal Society of Edinburgh*, vol. 3, pt. 1, pp. 55–137 [Edinburgh: The Society, 1794].)

147 Viner, Jacob. "Adam Smith and Laissez-faire." In *Adam Smith, 1776–1926 . . .*, by John M. Clark et al., pp. 116–55. Chicago: University of Chicago Press, 1928. Reprint ed., New York: Kelley, 1966.

148 Viner, Jacob. "Adam Smith and Laissez-faire." In *Essays in Economic*

Thought: Aristotle to Marshall, edited by Joseph J. Spengler and William R. Allen, pp. 305–29. Chicago: Rand McNally, 1960.

149   Viner, Jacob. "Adam Smith and Laissez-faire." In his *The Long View and the Short: Studies in Economic Theory and Policy,* pp. 213–45. Glencoe, Ill.: Free Press, 1958.

150   West, Edwin G. *Adam Smith.* New Rochelle, N.Y.: Arlington House, 1969.

151   West, Edwin G. *Adam Smith: The Man and His Works.* Indianapolis: Liberty Press, [1969], 1976.

152   Wilson, George W., ed. "*The Wealth of Nations,* by A. Smith." In his *Classics of Economic Theory.* Bloomington: Indiana University Press, 1964.

153   Withers, Hartley. "Adam Smith." In *From Anne to Victoria,* edited by Bonamy Dobrée, pp. 422–37. New York: Scribner's, 1937.

Methodology and the Nature of Inquiry

ARTICLES

154   Lindgren, J. Ralph. "Adam Smith's Theory of Inquiry." *Journal of Political Economy* 77 (November 1969): 897–915.

155   Meyers, M. L. "Adam Smith as Critic of Ideas." *Journal of the History of Ideas* 36 (April–June 1975): 281–96.

156   O'Brien, Denis P. "The Longevity of Adam Smith's Vision: Paradigms, Research Programmes, and Falsifiability in the History of Economic Thought." *Scottish Journal of Political Economy* 23 (June 1976): 133–51.

157   Pokorný, Dušan, "Smith and Walras: Two Theories of Science." *Canadian Journal of Economics* 11 (August 1978): 387–403.

158   Schumpeter, Joseph. "Science and Ideology." *American Economic Review* 39 (March 1949): 345–59.

159   Skinner, Andrew S. "Adam Smith: Philosophy and Science." *Scottish Journal of Political Economy* 29 (November 1972): 307–19.

160   Thompson, Herbert F. "Adam Smith's Philosophy of Science." *Quarterly Journal of Economics* 79 (May 1965): 212–33.

161   West, Edwin G. "Adam Smith and Alienation: A Rejoinder." *Oxford Economic Papers* 27, no. 2 (1975): 295–301.

162 Zurawicki, Sweryn A. "The Part of Adam Smith in the Development of Economic Thought." *Ekonomista* 5 (1976): 1025–45.

BOOKS

163 Deane, Phyllis. *The Evolution of Economic Ideas*. London: Cambridge University Press, 1978. (Commentary on Smith.)
164 Hollander, Samuel. "The Historical Dimension of the *Wealth of Nations*." In *Transactions of the Royal Society of Canada*, ser. 4, vol. 14, 1976, pp. 277–92. Ottowa: The Society, 1977.
165 Hutchinson, Terrance W. *On Revolutions and Progress in Economic Knowledge*. Cambridge, New York, and Melbourne: Cambridge University Press, 1978. (Various comments on the relation between economics and philosophy as found in Smith, Jevons, and Keynes.)
166 Taylor, Overton H. "Adam Smith's Philosophy of Science and Theory of Social Psychology and Ethics." In his *A History of Economic Thought*, pp. 49–76. New York: McGraw-Hill, 1960.
167 Wightman, William P. "Adam Smith and the History of Ideas." In *Essays on Adam Smith*, edited by Andrew S. Skinner and Thomas Wilson, pp. 44–67. Oxford: Clarendon Press, 1975.

Historical and Literary Research

ARTICLES

168 Bourne, Edward G. "Alexander Hamilton and Adam Smith." *Quarterly Journal of Economics* 8 (April 1894): 328–44.
169 Cannan, Edwin. "Two Letters of Adam Smith's." *Economic Journal* 8 (September 1898): 402–4.
170 Dankert, Clyde E. "Adam Smith and James Boswell." *Queen's Quarterly* 68 (1971): 323–32.
171 Dankert, Clyde E. "Two Eighteenth Century Celebrities." *Dalhousie Review* 42 (1962): 364–75.
172 Diamond, Sigmund. "Bunker Hill, Tory Propaganda, and Adam Smith." *New England Quarterly* 25 (September 1952): 363–74.
173 Dickinson, Z. Clark. "A Letter from Adam Smith." *Quarterly Journal of Economics* 72 (May 1958): 157–65.

174 Duncan, Elmer H., and Baird, Robert M. "Thomas Reid's Criticisms of Adam Smith's *Theory of Moral Sentiments*." *Journal of the History of Ideas* 38 (July-September 1977): 509–22.

175 Ferguson, Adam. "Of the Principle of Moral Estimation: A Discourse Between David Hume, Robert Clerk, and Adam Smith. An Unpublished Mss." Edited and with a foreword by Ernest C. Mossner. *Journal of the History of Ideas* 21 (April 1960): 222–32.

176 Gerber, J. C. "Emerson and the Political Economists." *New England Quarterly* 22 (September 1949): 238–46.

177 Gherity, James A. "A Quest for the Unrecognized Publication of Adam Smith." *Scottish Journal of Political Economy* 18 (February 1971):113–16.

178 Groenewegen, P. D. "Turgot and Adam Smith." *Scottish Journal of Political Ecomony* 16 (November 1969): 271–87.

179 Guttridge, G. H. "Adam Smith on the American Revolution: An Unpublished Memoir." *American Historical Review* 38 (July 1933): 714–20.

180 Hollander, Jacob H. "Adam Smith and James Anderson." *Annals of the American Academy of Political and Social Sciences* 7 (May 1896): 461–64.

181 Hollander, Samuel. "On Professor Samuelson's Canonical Classical Model of Political Economy." *Journal of Economic Literature* 18, no. 2 (1980): 559–78.

182 Jones, Reginald. "A Conjecture About Adam Smith." *Dalhousie Review* 18 (1938): 309–14.

183 Kirk, Russell. "Three Pillars of Order: Edmund Burke, Samul Johnson, Adam Smith." *Modern Age* 25, no. 3 (1981): 226–33.

184 La Nauze, John A. "A Manuscript Attributed to Adam Smith." *Economic Journal* 55 (June–September 1945): 288–91.

185 "A Letter of Adam Smith to Henry Dundas, 1789." [Edited by W. R. Scott] *Economic History Review* 3 (January 1931): 88–90.

186 Macfie, Alec. "The Invisible Hand of Jupiter." *Journal of the History of Ideas* 32 (October 1971): 595–99.

187 Meek, Ronald L. "New Light on Adam Smith's Glasgow Lectures on Jurisprudence." *History of Political Economy* 8 (Winter 1976): 439–77.

188 Middendorf, John H. "Dr. Johnson and Adam Smith." *Philological Quarterly* 40, no. 2 (April 1961): 281–96.

189 Nelson, John O. "Has the Authorship of the 'Abstract' Really Been Decided?" *Philosophical Quarterly* 26 (January 1976): 82–91.

190 Norton, D. F., and Stewart-Robertson, J. C. "Thomas Reid on Adam

Smith's Theory of Morals." *Journal of the History of Ideas* 41 (July–September 1980): 381–98.

191 Rae, John. "Letter of Adam Smith to the Duke of La Rochefoucauld." *Atheneum* 106 (December 28, 1895): 902.

192 Raphael, David D. "Adam Smith and the 'Infection' of David Hume's Society." *Journal of the History of Ideas* 30 (April 1969): 225–48.

193 Rogers, James E. T. "A Letter of Adam Smith [to William Pulteney, M.P.]. *Academy* 27 (February 28, 1885): 152.

194 Ross, Ian S., and Webster, A. M. "Adam Smith: Two Letters." *Scottish Journal of Political Economy* 28 (June 1981): 206–9.

195 Scott, William R. "Adam Smith and the Glasgow Merchants." *Economic Journal* 44 (September 1934): 506–8.

196 Scott, William R. "Adam Smith at Downing Street, 1766–67." *Economic History Review* 6 (October 1935): 79–89.

197 Scott, William R. "A Manuscript Criticism of *The Wealth of Nations* in 1776, by Hugh Blair." *Economic History* 4 (February 1938): 47–53.

198 Scott, William R. "The Manuscript of Adam Smith's Glasgow Lectures." *Economic History Review* 3 (January 1931): 91–92.

199 Scott, William R. "The Manuscript of an Early Draft of Part of *The Wealth of Nations*." *Economic Journal* 45 (September 1935): 427–38.

200 Sidgwick, Henry. "Letter to the Editor on Smith's 'Relation Between Local and Imperial Taxation.'" *Economic Journal* 5 (September 1895): 411–12.

201 Skinner, Andrew S. "Economics and History." *Scottish Journal of Political Economy* 12 (February 1965): 1–22.

202 Skinner, Andrew S. "Sir James Steuart: Author of a System." *Scottish Journal of Political Economy* 28, no. 1 (1981): 20–42.

203 Smith, Robert S. "The First Spanish Edition of the *Wealth of Nations*." *South African Journal of Economics* 35 (September 1967): 265–68.

204 "An Unpublished Letter of Adam Smith." *Economic Journal* 33 (September 1923): 427–28.

205 Vanderblue, Homer B. "An Incident in the Life of Adam Smith, Commissioner of His Majesty's Customs." *American Economic Review* 27 (June 1937): 305–8.

206 Willis, Kirk. "The Role in Parliament of the Economic Ideas of Adam Smith, 1776–1800." *History of Political Economy* 11 (Winter 1979): 505–44.

BOOKS

207 Black, R. D. Collison. "Smith's Contribution in Historical Perspective." In *The Market and the State: Essays in Honour of Adam Smith*, edited by Thomas Wilson and Andrew S. Skinner, pp. 42–63 (followed by Comments by D. P. O'Brien and D. N. Winch, pp. 67–72). Oxford: Clarendon Press, 1976.

208 Fay, Charles R. *Burke and Adam Smith, Being a Lecture Delivered at the Queen's University of Belfast, April 27, 1956*. Belfast: Queen's University, 1956.

209 Lundberg, I. C. *Turgot's Unknown Translator: The "Réflexions" and Adam Smith*. The Hague: Nijhoff, 1964.

210 Smith, Adam. *Four Autographed Letters of Adam Smith to Lord Hailes, 1769, Kircaldy*. Tokyo: Yushodo, 1968.

Smith's Place in the History of Political Economy

ARTICLES

211 Butler, R. J. "The Inaugural Address: T and Sympathy." *Aristotelian Society* 49 (1975): 1–20.

212 Cunningham, William. "The Progress of Economic Doctrine in England in the Eighteenth Century." *Economic Journal* 1 (March 1891): 73–94.

213 Gee, J. M. "Origin of Rent in Adam Smith's Wealth of Nations: An Anti-neoclassical View." *History of Political Economy* 13 (Spring 1981): 1–18.

214 Groenwegen, Peter D. "History and Political Economy: Smith, Marx, and Marshall." *Australian Economic Papers* 21 (June 1982): 1–17.

215 Kaufman, M. "Adam Smith and His Foreign Critics." *Scottish Review* 10 (1887): 387–411.

216 Meek, Ronald L. "Smith, Turgot, and the 'Four Stages' Theory." *History of Political Economy* 1 (June 1954): 138–53.

217 Mirowski, P. E. "Adam Smith, Empiricism, and the Rate of Profit in Eighteenth-century England." *History of Political Economy* 14 (Summer 1982): 178–98.

218 Nicholson, Joseph S. "The Reaction in Favor of the Classical Political Economy." *Journal of Political Economy* 2 (December 1893): 119–32.

219 "The Opinions of Ricardo and of Adam Smith on Some of the Leading Doctrines of Political Economy Stated and Compared." *Pamphleteer* 23 and 24 (1824).

220 Smith, Robert S. "The *Wealth of Nations*" in Spain and Hispanic America, 1780–1830." *Journal of Political Economy* 65 (April 1957): 104–25.

221 Taylor, William L. "Eighteenth Century Scottish Political Economy: The Impact on Adam Smith and His Work of His Association with Francis Hutcheson and David Hume." *South African Journal of Economics* 24 (December 1956): 261–76.

222 Veblen, Thorstein. "Preconceptions of Economic Science, I." *Quarterly Journal of Economics* 13 (January 1899): 121–50.

223 Veblen, Thorstein. "Preconceptions of Economic Science, II." *Quarterly Journal of Economics* 13 (July 1899): 396–426.

BOOKS

224 Boulding, Kenneth E. "Adam Smith as an Institutional Economist: The Frank E. Seidman Distinguished Award in Political Economy Acceptance Paper." Memphis, Tenn.: P. K. Seidman Foundation, 1976.

225 Boulding, Kenneth E. *Evolutionary Economics.* Beverly Hills, Calif.: Sage, 1981.

226 Hasek, Carl W. "The Introduction of Adam Smith's Doctrines into Germany." Ph.D. dissertation, Columbia University, 1925.

227 Hasek, Carl W. *The Introduction of Adam Smith's Doctrines into Germany.* Studies in History, Economics, and Public Law, vol. 117, no. 2, whole no. 261. New York: Columbia University Press, 1925.

228 Kobayashi, Noboru. *James Steuart, Adam Smith, and Friedrich List.* Science Council of Japan, Division of Economics, Commerce, and Business Administration, Economic series, no. 20. Tokyo: [Third Division, Science Council of Japan], 1967.

229 Meek, Ronald L. *Smith, Marx, and After: Ten Essays in the Development of Economic Thought.* New York: Wiley, 1977; London: Chapman & Hall.

230 Meek, Ronald L., ed. *Precursors of Adam Smith: Readings in Economic History and Theory.* London: Dent, 1973.

231 Palyi, Melchior. "The Introduction of Adam Smith on the Continent." In *Adam Smith, 1776–1926 . . . ,* by John M. Clark et al., pp. 180–225. Chicago: University of Chicago Press, 1928. Reprint ed., New York: Kelley, 1966.

232 Ramsay, John. *Scotland and Scotsmen in the Eighteenth Century.* 2 vols. Edited by Alexander Allardyce. Edinburgh: William Blackwell, 1880. Vol. 1, pp. 461–69.

233 Rechtenwald, Horst C., ed. *Political Economy: A Historical Perspective.* London: Collier-Macmillan, 1973. (Section on Smith.)

General Economic Theory

ARTICLES

234 Christensen, Paul P. "Sraffian Themes in Adam Smith's Theory." *Journal of Post Keynesian Economics* 2 (Fall 1979): 94–109.

235 Coats, Alfred W. "Beyond Adam Smith's Economics." *Kyklos* 32, no. 3 (1979): 603–5.

236 [De Quincey, Thomas.] "Ricardo Made Easy; or, What Is the Radical Difference Between Ricardo and Smith? With an Occasional Notice of Ricardo's Oversights. Part I." *Blackwood's Magazine* 52 (September 1842): 338–53.

237 [De Quincey, Thomas.] "Ricardo Made Easy; or, What Is the Radical Difference Between Ricardo and Smith? Part II." *Blackwood's Magazine* 52 (October 1842): 457–69.

238 [De Quincey, Thomas.] "Ricardo Made Easy; or, What Is the Radical Difference Between Ricardo and Smith? Part III." *Blackwood's Magazine* 52 (December 1842): 718–39.

239 Elliott, John E. "Social and Institutional Dimensions of the Theory of Capitalism in Classical Political Economy." *Journal of Economic Issues* 14 (June 1980): 473–92.

240 Gee, J. M. "Adam Smith's Social Welfare Function." *Scottish Journal of Political Economy* 15 (November 1968): 238–99.

241 Henderson, John P. "The Macro and Micro Aspects of the *Wealth of Nations.*" *Southern Economic Journal* 21 (July 1954): 25–35.

242 Hollander, Samuel. "Some Technological Relationships in the *Wealth*

of Nations and Ricardo's *Principles.*" *Canadian Journal of Economics* 32 (May 1966): 184–201.

243 Hoshino, Akio. "A System of Power in Adam Smith's Theory." *Kanto University Economic Review*, no. 1 (1978): 66–74.

244 Kurz, Heinz D. "Smithian Themes in Piero Sraffa's Theory." *Journal of Post Keynesian Economics* 3 (Winter 1980–81): 271–81.

245 MacDonald, Robert A. "Ricardo's Criticisms of Adam Smith." *Quarterly Journal of Economics* 26 (August 1912): 549–92.

246 Meyers, Milton L. "Adam Smith's Concept of Equilibrium." *Journal of Economic Issues* 10 (September 1976): 560–75.

247 Miller, William L. "Richard Jones's Contribution to the Theory of Rent." *History of Political Economy* 9, no. 3 (1977): 366–83.

248 Moos, S. "Is Adam Smith Out of Date?" *Oxford Economic Papers*, n.s. 3, (June 1951): 187–201.

249 Papola, T. S. "A 'Primitive' Equilibrium System: A Neglected Aspect of Smith's Economics." *Indian Journal of Economics* 17 (July–September 1969): 93–100.

250 Samuelson, Paul A. "A Modern Theorist's Vindication of Adam Smith." *American Economic Review* 67 (February 1977): 42–49.

251 Simpson, David. "Further Technological Relationships in *The Wealth of Nations* and in Ricardo's *Principles.*" *Canadian Journal of Economics and Politics* 33 (November 1967): 585–90.

252 Tame, Chris R. "Against the New Mercantilism: The Relevance of Adam Smith." *Il Politico* 43, no. 4 (1978): 766–75.

BOOKS

253 Bell, John F. "The *Wealth of Nations.*" In his *A History of Economic Thought*, pp. 167–91. New York: Ronald, 1953. (Extensive comments on Smith's economic analysis.)

254 Bladen, Vincent W. *From Adam Smith to Maynard Keynes: The Heritage of Political Economy*. Toronto: University of Toronto Press, 1974. (Book 1: "*Wealth of the Nations*," pp. 3–126.)

255 Blanqui, Jérôme A. *History of Political Economy in Europe*. Translated from the 4th French edition. New York: Putnam's, 1885. pp. 379–91.

256 Bowley, Marian. *Nassau Senior and Classical Economics*. London: Allen & Unwin, 1937. Reprint ed., New York: Octagon Books, 1967. (Comments on Adam Smith on pp. 67–74.)

257 Burtt, Everett J., Jr. *Social Perspectives in the History of Economic Theory*. New York: St. Martin's, 1972. (Comments on Smith's economic and social theories.)

258 Cannan, Edwin. *A History of Theories of Production and Distribution in English Political Economy from 1776 to 1848*. 3d ed., London: P. S. King, 1924. (Smith's economic theories are discussed on pp. 43–70.)

259 Catherwood, Benjamin F. "Adam Smith." In his *Basic Theories of Distribution*, pp. 20–58. London: P. S. King, 1939.

260 Clark, John M. "Adam Smith and the Currents of History." In *Adam Smith, 1776–1926 . . .* , by John M. Clark et al., pp. 53–76. Chicago: University of Chicago Press, 1928. Reprint ed., New York: Kelley, 1966.

261 De Wilson, F. A. B. *Analysis of Adam Smith's "Wealth of Nations."* 2 vols. Oxford: A. T. Shrimpton, 1885.

262 Dobb, Maurice H. "Ricardo and Adam Smith." In *Essays on Adam Smith*, edited by Andrew S. Skinner and Thomas Wilson, pp. 324–35. Oxford: Clarendon Press, 1975.

263 Haney, Lewis H. "Adam Smith . . . " In his *History of Economic Thought*, pp. 193–225. New York: Macmillan Co. 1927.

264 Harrison, Frederick. "Is It Consistent with the Design and Practice of Adam Smith to Treat the Laws of Industry as an Independent and Abstract Science?" Address [before the Political Economy Club, London, February 1, 1878.] London: Political Economy Club, 1881.

265 Hollander, Samuel. *The Economics of Adam Smith*. Toronto: Toronto University Press [1973], 1976.

266 Ingram, John K. "Third Modern Phase: System of Natural Liberty." In his *A History of Political Economy*, 2d ed., pp. 87–110. London: A. & C. Black, 1910.

267 Leake, Percy D. *Capital: Adam Smith, Karl Marx*. The Accountant Lecture Series. London: Gee & Co., 1933.

268 Morrow, Glenn R. "The Economics and Economic Theories of Adam Smith: A Study of Social Conceptions in the Eighteenth Century." Ph.D. dissertation, Cornell University, 1921.

269 Rogin, Leo. "Adam Smith." In his *The Meaning and Validity of Economic Theory*, pp. 51–109. New York: Harper, 1956.

270 Spengler, Joseph J., and Allen, William R. ed. *Essays in Economic Thought, Aristotle to Marshall*, Chicago: Rand McNally, 1960. Pp. 288–329. (Reprints of articles by H. M. Robertson and W. L. Taylor.)

271 Spiegel, Henry W. *The Growth of Economic Thought.* Englewood Cliffs, N.J.: Prentice-Hall, 1971. Pp. 221–64.

272 Taylor, Overton H. "Adam Smith's Ideal and Theory of the Self-adjusting Liberal Economy." In his *A History of Economic Thought*, pp. 77–117. New York: McGraw-Hill, 1960.

Price and Distribution Theory

ARTICLES

273 Bladen, Vincent W. "Adam Smith on Productive and Unproductive Labour: A Theory of Full Development." *Canadian Journal of Economics and Politics* 26 (November 1960): 625–30.

274 Bladen, Vincent W. "Command over Labour: A Study in Misinterpretation." *Canadian Journal of Economics* 8 (November 1975): 504–19.

275 Blaug, Mark. "Welfare Indices in the *Wealth of Nations.*" *Southern Economic Journal* 26 (October 1959): 150–53.

276 Das Gupta, A. K. "Adam Smith on Value." *Indian Economic Review* 5 (August 1960): 105–15.

277 Das Gupta, A. K. "A Postscript." *Indian Economic Review* 5 (February 1961): 285–87.

278 Douglas, Paul H. "Adam Smith's Theory of Value and Distribution." *University Journal of Business* 5 (January 1927): 53–104.

279 Hla Myint, U. "The Welfare Significance of Productive Labour." *Review of Economic Studies* (Winter 1943): 20–30.

280 Kaushil, S. "The Case of Adam Smith's Value Analysis." *Oxford Economic Papers* 25 (March 1973): 60–71.

281 Larsen, Robert M. "Adam Smith's Theory of Market Prices." *Indian Economic Journal* 24 (January–March 1977): 219–35.

282 Larsen, Robert M. "Adam Smith's Theory of Production and Distribution." *Intermountain Economic Review* 9 (Spring 1978): 38–50.

283 Larsen, Robert M. "Dmitriev's Smithian Model." *Scottish Journal of Political Economy* 24 (November 1977): 227–33.

284 McNulty, Paul J. "A Note on the History of Perfect Competition." *Journal of Political Economy* 75 (August 1967): 395–99.

285 Meek, Ronald L. "Value in the History of Economic Thought." *History of Political Economy* 6 (Fall 1974): 246–60. (Smith's views

are covered chiefly on pp. 252–58.)

286 Robertson, Hector M., and Taylor, William L. "Adam Smith's Approach to the Theory of Value." *Economic Journal* 67 (June 1957): 181–98.

287 Thweatt, William O. "Early Formulators of Say's Law." *Quarterly Review of Economics and Business* 19 (Winter 1979): 79–96.

BOOKS

288 Bladen, Vincent W. "Adam Smith on Value." In *Essays in Political Economy in Honour of E. J. Urwick*, edited by H. A. Innis, pp. 27–43. Toronto: University of Toronto Press, 1938.

289 Cannan, Edwin. "Adam Smith's Cost of Production Theory." In his *A Review of Economic Theory*, pp. 164–72. London: King, 1929.

290 Cotterill, Charles F. *An Examination of the Doctrines of Value, as Set Forth by Adam Smith, Ricardo, McCulloch, Mill, etc.* London: Simpkin & Marshall, 1831.

291 Dobb, Maurice H. "Adam Smith." In his *Theories of Value and Distribution Since Adam Smith: Ideology and Economic Theory*, pp. 38–64. Cambridge: Cambridge University Press, 1973.

292 Douglas, Paul H. "Smith's Theory of Value and Distribution." In *Adam Smith 1776–1926 . . .* , by John M. Clark et al., pp. 77–115. Chicago: University of Chicago Press, 1928. Reprint ed., New York: Kelley, 1966.

293 Heimann, Eduard. "Economics as Physics—Adam Smith." In his *History of Economic Doctrines: An Introduction to Economic Theory*, pp. 63–76. New York and London: Oxford University Press, 1945.

294 Hla Myint, U. *Theories of Welfare Economics*. Cambridge, Mass.: Harvard University Press, 1948. Reprint ed., New York: Kelley, 1965.

295 Hollander, Samuel. "The Role of Utility and Demand in *The Wealth of Nations*." In *Essays on Adam Smith*, edited by Andrew S. Skinner and Thomas Wilson, pp. 313–23. Oxford: Clarendon Press, 1975.

296 Labini-Sylos, P. "Competition: The Product Markets." In *The Market and the State: Essays in Honour of Adam Smith*, edited by Thomas Wilson and Andrew S. Skinner, pp. 200–32 (followed by comments by C. K. Rowley and A. Nove, pp. 232–42). Oxford: Clar-

endon Press, 1976.

297 Larsen, Robert M. "Adam Smith's Theory of Value and Distribution." Ph.D. dissertation, University of California, Riverside, 1976.

298 Meek, Ronald L. "Adam Smith and the Development of the Labour Theory." In his *Studies in the Labour Theory of Value*. 2d ed. New York: Monthly Review Press, 1980.

299 Richardson, George B. "Adam Smith on Competition and Increasing Returns." In *Essays on Adam Smith*, edited by Andrew S. Skinner and Thomas Wilson, pp. 350–60. Oxford: Clarendon Press, 1975.

300 Robbins, Lionel. *Robert Torrens and the Evolution of Classical Economics*. New York: St. Martin's, 1958. (A substantial portion of Torrens' work was concerned with the theories of production, distribution, and value as they had been stated by Adam Smith.)

301 Schneider, George E. "Resource Allocation and the Beginnings of Welfare Economics in Adam Smith's Theory of Economic Policy." Ph.D. dissertation, University of Notre Dame, 1969.

302 Walsh, Vivian, and Gram, Harvey. *Classical and Neoclassical Theories of General Equilibrium: Historical Origins and Mathematical Structure*. New York and Oxford: Oxford University Press, 1980. (Surveys models and theories of general equilibrium found in the works of Smith and other early economists.)

303 Walton, Paul. *From Alienation to Surplus Value*. London: Sheed & Ward, 1972.

304 Whitaker, Albert. *History and Criticism of the Labor Theory of Value in English Political Economy*. New York: Columbia University Press, 1904. Pp. 16–40.

305 Williams, Philip L. *The Emergence of the Theory of the Firm: From Adam Smith to Alfred Marshall*. New York: St. Martin's, 1978. Pp. 11–39.

306 Wolf, Edward N. "Models of Production and Exchange in the Thought of Adam Smith and David Ricardo." Ph.D. dissertation, Yale University, 1974.

307 Young, Jeffrey T. *Classical Theories of Value: From Smith to Sraffa*. Boulder, Colo.: Westview Press, 1978.

Economic Growth and Development

ARTICLES

308 Anspach, Ralph. "Smith's Growth Paradigm." *History of Political Economy* 8 (Winter 1976): 494–514.

309 Avila, Manuel. "Smith and Undeveloped [sic] Nations." *Review of Social Economy* 34 (December 1976): 345–58. (Title page reads "Undeveloped." Errata slip states that "Undeveloped" should read "Underdeveloped.")

310 Barkai, Haim, "A Formal Outline of a Smithian Growth Model." *Quarterly Journal of Economics* 83 (August 1969): 396–414.

311 Brenner, R. "Origins of Capitalist Development: A Critique of Neo-Smithian Marxism." *New Left Review*, no. 104 (July 1977): 25–92.

312 Chaudhuri, Asoke K. "The *Wealth of Nations* and Underdeveloped Countries." *Asian Economic Review* 1 (August 1959): 415–31.

313 Cullison, W. E. "Examining the Effect of Interdependent Consumer Preferences on Economic Growth, or Re-discovering Adam Smith and His Eighteenth Century Contemporaries." *Southern Economic Journal* 44 (April 1978): 937–44.

314 Hollander, Samuel. "Some Implications of Adam Smith's Analysis of Investment Priorities." *History of Political Economy* 3 (Fall 1971): 245–64.

315 Khan, Mohammed. "Adam Smith's Theory of Economic Development (in Relation to Underdeveloped Economies)." *Indian Journal of Economics* 34 (April 1954): 337–42.

316 Lockwood, William W. "Adam Smith and Asia." *Journal of Asian Studies* 23 (May 1964): 345–55.

317 Lowe, Adolph. "The Classical Theory of Economic Growth." *Social Research* 21 (Summer 1954): 132–41.

318 Robertson, Hector M. "Euge! Belle! Dear Mr. Smith: *The Wealth of Nations, 1776–1976*." *South African Journal of Economics* 44 (December 1976): 378–411.

319 Rosenberg, Nathan. "Some Institutional Aspects of the *Wealth of the Nations*." *Journal of Political Economy* 68 (December 1960): 557–70.

320 Singh, V. B. "Adam Smith's Theory of Economic Development." *Science and Society* 23 (Spring 1959): 107–32.

321 Spengler, Joseph J. "Adam Smith on Population Growth and Economic Development." *Population and Development Review* 2 (June 1976): 167–80.

322 Spengler, Joseph J. "Adam Smith's Theory of Economic Growth, Part I." *Southern Economic Journal* 25 (April 1959): 397–415.

323 Spengler, Joseph J. "Adam Smith's Theory of Economic Growth, Part II." *Southern Economic Journal* 26 (July 1959): 1–12.

324 Thweatt, William O. "A Diagrammatic Presentation of Adam Smith's

Growth Model." *Social Research* 24 (Summer 1957): 227–30.

325 Zweig, Konrad. "Yesterday's Predictions: Smith, Malthus, Ricardo, and Mill: The Forerunners of Limits to Growth." *Futures* 11 (December 1979): 510–23.

BOOKS

326 Adelman, Irma. *Theories of Economic Growth and Development.* Stanford, Calif.: Stanford University Press, 1961. Pp. 25–42.

327 Bowley, Marian. "Some Aspects of the Treatment of Capital in *The Wealth of Nations.*" In *Essays on Adam Smith,* edited by Andrew S. Skinner and Thomas Wilson, pp. 361–76. Oxford: Clarendon Press, 1975.

328 Chaudhuri, Asoke. *The "Wealth of Nations": An Analysis with Special Reference to Under-Developed Countries.* Calcutta: World Press, 1967.

329 Eltis, Walter A. "Adam Smith's Theory of Economic Growth." In *Essays on Adam Smith,* edited by Andrew S. Skinner and Thomas Wilson, pp. 426–54. Oxford: Clarendon Press, 1975.

330 Hartwell, R. N. "Adam Smith and the Industrial Revolution." In *Adam Smith and "The Wealth of Nations": 1776–1976,* edited by Fred R. Glahe, pp. 123–47. Boulder, Colo.: Colorado Associated University Press, 1978.

331 Letiche, J. M. "Adam Smith and David Ricardo on Economic Growth." In *Theories of Economic Growth,* by Berthold Hoselitz et al., pp. 65–88. Glencoe, Ill.: Free Press, 1960.

332 Lewis, W. Arthur. "The Diffusion of Development." In *The Market and the State: Essays in Honour of Adam Smith,* edited by Thomas Wilson and Andrew S. Skinner, pp. 135–56 (followed by comments by H. L. Myint and I. G. Stewart, pp. 156–63). Oxford: Clarendon Press, 1976.

333 Lowe, Adolph. "Adam Smith's System of Equilibrium Growth." In *Essays on Adam Smith,* edited by Andrew S. Skinner and Thomas Wilson, pp. 415–25. Oxford: Clarendon Press, 1975.

International Economics

ARTICLES

334 "Adam Smith on Prohibitory Duties, Text of a Letter to William Eden." *Nation* 62 (January 30, 1896): 98.

335 Ashley, William. "A Retrospect of Free Trade Doctrine." *Economic Journal* 34 (December 1924): 501–39.

336 Chaudhuri, Asoke K. "Adam Smith on International Economics." *Asian Economic Review* 2 (May 1960): 366–77.

337 Eagly, Robert V. "Adam Smith and the Specie-Flow Doctrine." *Scottish Journal of Political Economy* 17 (February 1970): 61–68.

338 Fay, Charles R. "Adam Smith and Foreign Trade." *Southwestern Political and Social Science Quarterly* 8 (March 1928): 338–43.

339 Hla Myint, U. "Adam Smith's Theory of International Trade in the Perspective of Economic Development." *Economica* 44 (August 1977): 231–48.

340 La Nauze, John A. "The Substance of Adam Smith's Attack on Mercantilism." *Economic Record* 13 (June 1937): 90–93.

341 Mitchell, A. A. "A Retrospect of Free-trade Doctrine." *Economic Journal* 35 (June 1925): 214–20.

342 Petrella, Frank. "Adam Smith's Rejection of Hume's Price-Specie-Flow Mechanism: A Minor Mystery Resolved." *Southern Economic Journal* 34 (January 1968): 365–74.

343 Staley, Charles E. "A Note on Adam Smith's Version of the Vent for Surplus Model." *History of Political Economy* 5, no. 2 (1973): 438–48.

BOOKS

344 Bloomfield, Arthur I. "Adam Smith and the Theory of International Trade." In *Essays on Adam Smith,* edited by Andrew S. Skinner and Thomas Wilson, pp. 455–81. Oxford: Clarendon Press, 1975.

345 Bonar, James. *Adam Smith . . . The Revolutionary Element in Adam Smith.* London: P. S. King & Son, 1924(?). ("The first of a course of addresses on 'Pioneers of Free Trade,' given at the National Liberal Club, Political and Economic Circle, 30 January 1924.")

346 Cunningham, William. *Richard Cobden and Adam Smith: Two Lectures*. London: Tariff Reform League, 1904.

347 Douglas, Roy. *Land Reform in the British Isles and Adam Smith and Free Trade*. London: International Union for Land-value Taxation and Free Trade, 1974.

348 Earle, Edward M., ed. "Adam Smith, Alexander Hamilton, Friedrich List: The Economic Foundations of Military Power." In his *Makers of Modern Strategy*, pp. 117–54. Princeton: Princeton University Press, 1943. (Smith is covered mainly in pp. 117–28.)

349 Fleming, J. Marcus. "Mercantilism and Free Trade Today." In *The Market and the State: Essays in Honour of Adam Smith*, edited by Thomas Wilson and Andrew S. Skinner, pp. 164–85 (followed by comments by H. Giersch and W. M. Corden, pp. 185–99). Oxford: Clarendon Press, 1976.

350 Heckscher, Eli F. *Mercantilism*. Translated by Mendel Shapiro. Rev. 2d ed. Edited by E. F. Söderlund. New York: Macmillan Co.; London: Allen & Unwin, 1935, 1955. (Numerous references to Smith's approach to international trade.)

351 Hirst, Francis W. "Adam Smith and Pitt." In his *From Adam Smith to Philip Snowden: A History of Free Trade in Britain*, pp. 1–10. London: Unwin, 1925.

352 McCord, Norman, comp. *Free Trade: Theory and Practice from Adam Smith to Keynes*. New York: Barnes & Noble, 1970. Pp. 16–39. (Condensations of passages from *Wealth of Nations*.)

353 Nicholson, Joseph S. *A Project of Empire: A Critical Study of the Economics of Imperialism, with Special Reference to the Ideas of Adam Smith*. London: Macmillan & Co., 1909.

354 Rae, John. *Statement of Some New Principles on the Subject of Political Economy, Exposing the Fallacies of the System of Free Trade and Some of the Other Doctrines Maintained in the "Wealth of the Nations."* Boston: Hillard, Gray, 1834.

Profits and Interest

ARTICLES

355 Meek, Ronald L. "Adam Smith and the Classical Concept of Profit." *Scottish Journal of Political Economy* 1 (June 1954): 138–53. (Reprinted in his *Economics and Ideology and Other Essays*, 1967.)

356 Ranadive, K. R. "*The Wealth of Nations*—The Vision and the Conceptualization." *Indian Economic Journal* 24 (January–March 1977): 295–332.

357 Rosenberg, Nathan. "Adam Smith on Profits—Paradox Lost and Regained." *Journal of Political Economy* 82 (November–December 1974): 1177–90.

BOOKS

358 Meek, Ronald L. "Adam Smith and the Classical Theory of Profit." In his *Economics and Ideology and Other Essays: Studies in the Development of Economic Thought*, pp. 18–33. London: Chapman & Hall, 1967.

359 Rosenberg, Nathan. "Adam Smith on Profits—Paradox Lost and Regained." In *Essays on Adam Smith*, edited by Andrew S. Skinner and Thomas Wilson, pp. 377–89. Oxford: Clarendon Press, 1975.

360 Tucker, G. S. L. "The Transition: Adam Smith." In his *Progress and Profits in British Economic Thought, 1650–1850*, pp. 49–73. Cambridge Studies in Economic History. Cambridge: Cambridge University Press, 1960.

Monetary Theory and Policy

ARTICLES

361 Hollander, Jacob H. "The Development of the Theory of Money from Adam Smith to David Ricardo." *Quarterly Journal of Economics* 25 (May 1911): 429–70.

362 Jadlow, J. M. "Adam Smith on Usury Laws." *Journal of Finance* 32 (September 1977): 1195–1200.

363 Laidler, D. "Adam Smith as a Monetary Economist." *Canadian Journal of Economics* 14 (May 1981): 185–200.

BOOKS

364 Checkland, Sydney G. "Adam Smith and the Bankers." In *Essays on Adam Smith*, edited by Andrew S. Skinner and Thomas Wilson, pp. 504–23. Oxford: Clarendon Press, 1975.

365 Horton, Samuel D. *The Parity of Moneys as Regarded by Adam Smith,*

Ricardo, and Mill. London: Macmillan & Co., 1888.

366 Poor, Henry V. "Adam Smith." In his *Money and Its Laws*, pp. 99–171. New York: H. V. and H. W. Poor, 1877.

367 Vickers, Douglas. "Adam Smith and the Status of the Theory of Money." In *Essays on Adam Smith*, edited by Andrew S. Skinner and Thomas Wilson, pp. 482–503. Oxford: Clarendon Press, 1975.

Labor Economics

ARTICLES

368 Henry, J. F. "Productive Labour, Exploitation, and Oppression—A Perspective." *Australian Economic Papers* 14 (June 1975): 35–40.

369 Lewis, T. J. "Adam Smith: The Labor Market as the Basis of Natural Right." *Journal of Economic Literature* 11 (March 1977): 21–50.

370 McNulty, Paul J. "Adam Smith's Concept of Labor." *Journal of the History of Ideas* 34 (July 1973): 345–66.

371 Miller, William L. "Adam Smith on Wage Differentials Against Agricultural Laborers." *Atlantic Economic Journal* 9 (July 1981): 19–24.

372 Temperley, Howard. "Capitalism, Slavery, and Ideology." *Past and Present* 75 (1977): 94–118.

BOOKS

373 Brown, E. H. Phelps. "The Labour Market." In *The Market and the State: Essays in Honour of Adam Smith*, edited by Thomas Wilson and Andrew S. Skinner, pp. 243–60 (followed by comments by L. C. Hunter and D. I. Mackay, pp. 260–70). Oxford: Clarendon Press, 1976.

374 Ginsberg, Eli. "Adam Smith as Management Theorist." In *The Business System: A Bicentennial View*, by Milton Friedman et al., pp. 41–51. Hanover, N.H.: Amos Tuck School of Business Administration; distributed by the University Press of New England, 1977.

375 Rees, Albert. "Compensating Wage Differentials." In *Essays on Adam*

Smith, edited by Andrew S. Skinner and Thomas Wilson, pp. 336–49. Oxford: Clarendon Press, 1975.

Division of Labor

ARTICLES

376 Foley, Vernard. "The Division of Labor in Plato and Smith." *History of Political Economy* 6 (Summer 1974): 220–42.

377 Friedson, E. "Division of Labor as Social Interaction." *Social Problems* 23 (February 1976): 304–13.

378 Groenewegen, P. D. "Adam Smith and the Division of Labour: A Bicentenary Estimate." *Australian Economic Papers* 16 (December 1977): 161–74.

379 Hamowy, Ronald. "Adam Smith, Adam Ferguson, and the Division of Labour." *Economica*, n.s., 35 (August 1968): 249–59.

380 Lamb, Robert B. "Adam Smith's Concept of Alienation." *Oxford Economic Papers* 25 (July 1973): 275–85.

381 McNulty, Paul J. "A Note on the Division of Labor in Plato and Smith." *History of Political Economy* 7 (Fall 1975): 372–78.

382 Meek, Ronald L., and Skinner, Andrew S. "The Development of Adam Smith's Ideas on the Division of Labour." *Economic Journal* 83 (December 1973): 1094–1116.

383 Myers, Milton M. "Division of Labour as a Principle of Social Cohesion." *Canadian Journal of Economics and Political Science* 33 (August 1967): 432–40. (Smith is discussed, along with other eighteenth-century writers.)

384 Rosenberg, Nathan. "Adam Smith on the Division of Labour: Two Views or One?" *Economica*, n.s., 32 (May 1965): 127–39.

385 Rosenberg, Nathan. "Another Advantage of the Division of Labor." *Journal of Political Economy* 84 (August 1976): 861–68.

386 Stigler, George J. "The Division of Labor Is Limited by the Extent of the Market." *Journal of Political Economy* 59 (June 1951); 185–93.

387 Weiss, D. D. "Marx Versus Smith on the Division of Labor." *Monthly Review* 28 (July 1976): 104–18.

388 West, Edwin G. "Adam Smith's Two Views on the Division of Labour." *Economica*, n.s., 31 (February 1964): 2–32.

389 West, Edwin G. "The Political Economy of Alienation: Karl Marx

and Adam Smith." *Oxford Economic Papers* 21 (March 1969): 1–23.

BOOKS

390 Adiseshiah, Malcolm S. *Some Thoughts on Adam Smith's Theory of the Division of Labour.* Ramasway Mudeliar Lectures, 1976. Trivandrum, India: Department of Publications, University of Kerala, 1977.
391 Meek, Ronald L. "Adam Smith and the Division of Labour." In his *Studies in the Labour Theory of Value*, 2d ed., pp. 45–81. New York and London: Monthly Review Press, 1976.
392 Price, Langford L. "Adam Smith: The Division of Labour." In his *A Short History of Political Economy in England*, pp. 1–34. London: Methuen, 1891.
393 West, Edwin G. "Adam Smith and Alienation: Wealth Increases, Men Decay?" In *Essays on Adam Smith*, edited by Andrew S. Skinner and Thomas Wilson, pp. 540–52. Oxford: Clarendon Press, 1975.

Public Finance

ARTICLES

394 Cannan, Edwin. "Adam Smith on Twentieth Century Finance." *Economica* 3 (June 1923): 93–97.
395 Lynn, Arthur D., Jr. "Adam Smith's Fiscal Ideas: An Eclectic Revisited." *National Tax Journal* 29 (December 1976): 369–78.
396 Nicholson, Joseph S. "Adam Smith on Public Debts." *Economic Journal* 30 (March 1920): 1–12.

BOOKS

397 Matthews, C. O. "Public Policy and Monetary Expenditure." In *The Market and the State: Essays in Honour of Adam Smith*, edited by Thomas Wilson and Andrew S. Skinner, pp. 330–45 (followed by comments by R. A. Gordon and R. Sayres, pp. 345–50). Oxford: Clarendon Press, 1976.

398 Musgrave, Richard A. "Adam Smith on Public Finance and Distribu-
     tion." In *The Market and the State: Essays in Honour of Adam
     Smith*, edited by Thomas Wilson and Andrew S. Skinner, pp. 296–
     319 (followed by comments by A. R. Prest and A. B. Atkinson,
     pp. 319–29). Oxford: Clarendon Press, 1976.
399 Peacock, Alan T. "The Treatment of the Principles of Public Finance
     in *The Wealth of Nations*." In *Essays on Adam Smith*, edited by
     Andrew S. Skinner and Thomas Wilson, pp. 553–67. Oxford:
     Clarendon Press, 1975.

Free Markets and Regulation of the Economy

ARTICLES

400 Grampp, William D. "Adam Smith and the Economic Man." *Journal
     of Political Economy* 56 (August 1948): 315–36.
401 Hollander, Samuel. "Adam Smith and the Self-interest Axiom." *Jour-
     nal of Law and Economics* 20 (April 1977): 133–52.
402 Kittrell, Edward. "Laissez-faire in English Classical Economics." *Jour-
     nal of the History of Ideas* 27 (October–December 1966): 610–
     20.
403 Knight, Frank H. "Laissez-faire, Pro and Con." *Journal of Political
     Economy* 75 (December 1967): 782–95.
404 Macfie, Alec. "The Moral Justification of Free Enterprise: A Lay Ser-
     mon on an Adam Smith Text." *Scottish Journal of Political Econ-
     omy* 14 (February 1967): 1–11.
405 Mumy, Gene E. "Town and Country in Adam Smith's *The Wealth of
     Nations*." *Science and Society* 2 (Winter 1978–79): 458–77.
406 Naggar, Tahaney. "Adam Smith's Laissez Faire." *American Economist*
     21 (Fall 1977): 35–39.
407 "Nations of Wealth." *Economist* 247 (June 2, 1973): 14 +.
408 Rashid, S. "Policy of Laissez-faire During Scarcities." *Economic Jour-
     nal* 90 (September 1980): 493–503.
409 Stigler, George J. "Perfect Competition Historically Contemplated."
     Journal of Political Economy 65 (February 1957): 1–17. (Smith's
     views are described mainly on pp. 1–3.)
410 West, Edwin G. "Adam Smith's Economics of Politics." *History of
     Political Economy* 8 (Winter 1976): 515–39.

411 West, Edwin G. "Burdens of Monopoly: Classical Versus Neoclassical." *Southern Economic Journal* 44 (April 1978): 829–45.

BOOKS

412 Baumol, William J. "Smith Versus Marx on Business Morality and the Social Interest." In *Adam Smith and the "Wealth of Nations": 1776–1976*, edited by Fred R. Glahe, pp. 111–22. Boulder, Colo.: Colorado Associated University Press, 1978.

413 Cairncross, Alexander. "The Market and the State." In *The Market and the State: Essays in Honour of Adam Smith*, edited by Thomas Wilson and Andrew S. Skinner, pp. 113–34. Oxford: Clarendon Press, 1976.

414 Coats, Alfred W. "Adam Smith and the Mercantile System." In *Essays on Adam Smith*, edited by Andrew S. Skinner and Thomas Wilson, pp. 218–36. Oxford: Clarendon Press, 1975.

415 Frankel, S. Herbert. *Adam Smith's "Invisible Hand" in a Velvet Glove.* Washington, D.C.: American Enterprise Institute for Public Policy Research, 1980.

416 Friedman, Milton. "Adam Smith's Relevance for 1976." International Institution for Economics Research. Los Angeles: The Institution, 1976.

417 Friedman, Milton et al. "Adam Smith's Relevance for 1976." In *Adam Smith and "The Wealth of Nations": 1776–1976*, edited by Fred R. Glahe, pp. 7–20. Boulder, Colo.: Colorado Associated University Press, 1978.

418 Johnson, Harry G. "The Individual and the State: Some Contemporary Problems." In *Adam Smith and the "Wealth of Nations": 1776–1976* , edited by Fred R. Glahe, pp. 21–34. Boulder, Colo.: Colorado Associated University Press, 1978.

419 Spengler, Joseph J. "Smith Versus Hobbes: Economy Versus Polity." In *Adam Smith and the "Wealth of Nations": 1776–1976*, edited by Fred R. Glahe, pp. 35–59. Boulder, Colo.: Colorado Associated University Press, 1978.

Technological Change

ARTICLES

420 Hoar, W. P. "The Industrial Revolution and the Free Market." *American Opinion* 23 (January 1980): 11–18 +.

421 Koebner, Richard. "Adam Smith and the Industrial Revolution." *Economic History Review* 11 (April 1959): 381–91.

422 Wrigley, E. A. "The Process of Modernization and Industrial Revolution in England." *Journal of Interdisciplinary History* 3, no. 2 (1972): 225–60.

BOOKS

423 Blaug, Mark. "Adam Smith and the Industrial Revolution." In his *Economic Theory in Retrospect*, 3d ed., pp. 36–68. Cambridge: Cambridge University Press, 1978. (Contains "Readers' Guide to the *Wealth of the Nations*.")

424 Kindleberger, Charles P. "The Historical Background: Adam Smith and the Industrial Revolution." In *The Market and the State: Essays in Honour of Adam Smith*, edited by Thomas Wilson and Andrew S. Skinner, pp. 1–25 (followed by comments by Asa Briggs and R. M. Hartwell, pp. 25–41.) Oxford: Clarendon Press, 1976.

425 Wisman, Jon D. "The Role of Technology in Economic Thought: Adam Smith to John Maynard Keynes." Ph.D. dissertation, American University, 1974.

War and Defense

ARTICLES

426 Bullock, Charles J. "Adam Smith's Views on National Defence." *Military Historian and Economist* 1 (1916): 249–57.

427 Neimanis, George J. "Militia vs. the Standing Army in the History of Economic Thought from Adam Smith to Friedrich Engels." *Military Affairs* 44, no. 1 (1980): 29–32.

428 Staley, Charles E. "Adam Smith and the Viet Nam War." *Atlantic Economic Journal* 1 (November 1973): 39–45.

BOOKS

429 Bullock, Charles J. "Adam Smith's Views on National Defence." In his *Economic Essays*, pp. 121–29. Cambridge, Mass.: Harvard University Press, 1936.

Philosophy and Moral Philosophy

ARTICLES

430 Anspach, Ralph. "The Implications of the *Theory of Moral Sentiments* for Adam Smith's Economic Thought." *History of Political Economy* 4 (Spring 1972): 176–206.

431 Billet, Leonard. "The Just Economy: The Moral Basis of the *Wealth of Nations.*" *Review of Social Economy* 34 (December 1976): 295–315.

432 Bonar, James. "The *Theory of Moral Sentiments* by Adam Smith, 1759." *Journal of Philosophic Studies* 1 (July 1926): 333–53.

433 Branson, Roy. "James Madison and the Scottish Enlightenment." *Journal of the History of Ideas* 40 (April–June 1979): 235–50.

434 Buchanan, James M. "The Justice of Natural Liberty." *Journal of Legal Studies* 5 (January 1976): 1–16.

435 Campbell, William F. "Adam Smith's Theory of Justice, Prudence, and Beneficence." *American Economic Review* 57 (May 1967): 571–77.

436 Checkland, Sydney G. "Growth and Progress: The Nineteenth Century View in Britain." *Economic History Review* 12 (August 1959): 49–62.

437 Coase, Ronald H. "Adam Smith's View of Man." *Journal of Law and Economics* 19 (October 1976): 529–46.

438 Danner, Peter L. "Sympathy and Exchangeable Value: Keys to Adam Smith's Social Philosophy." *Review of Social Economy* 34 (December 1976): 317–31.

439 Dunn, William C. "Adam Smith and Edmund Burke: Complementary Contemporaries." *Southern Economic Journal* 7 (January 1941): 330–46.

440 Fiering, Norman S. "Irresistible Compassion: An Aspect of Eighteenth-century Sympathy and Humanitarianism." *Journal of the History of Ideas* 37 (April–June 1976): 195–218.

441 Flew, Anthony. "Three Questions About Justice in the 'Treatise.' " *Philosophical Quarterly* 26 (January 1976): 1–13.

442 Foley, Vernard. "Smith and the Greeks: A Reply to Professor McNulty's Comments." *History of Political Economy* 7 (Fall 1975): 379–89.

443 Gill, Emily R. "Justice in Adam Smith: The Right and the Good." *Review of Social Economy* 34 (December 1976): 275–94.

444 Goss, Barry A. "Adam Smith on Abstinence." *Australian Economic Papers* 19 (June 1980): 16–21.

445 Grampp, William D. "Classical Economics and Its Moral Critics." *History of Political Economy* 5 (Fall 1973): 359–74.

446 Hamowy, Ronald. "Jefferson and the Scottish Enlightenment: A Critique of Garry Wills's Inventing America: Jefferson's Declaration of Independence." *William and Mary Quarterly* 36, no. 4 (1979): 503–23.

447 Harsanyi, John C. "Morality and the Theory of Rational Behavior." *Social Research* 44 (Winter 1977): 623–56.

448 Larmore, C. "Moral Judgment." *Review of Metaphysics* 35, no. 2 (1981): 275–96.

449 Levy, David. "Adam Smith's 'Natural Law' and Contractual Society." *Journal of the History of Ideas* 39 (October–December 1978): 665–74.

450 Macfie, Alec. "Adam Smith's *Theory of Moral Sentiments.*" *Scottish Journal of Political Economy* 8 (February 1961): 12–27.

451 McGill, A. D. "Theory and Experience in Adam Smith." *Journal of the History of Ideas* 36 (January–March 1975): 76–94.

452 MacLean, Kenneth. "Imagination and Sympathy: Sterne and Adam Smith." *Journal of the History of Ideas* 10 (June 1949): 399–410.

453 Morrow, Glenn R. "Adam Smith: Moralist and Philosopher." *Journal of Political Economy* 35 (June 1927): 321–42.

454 Morrow, Glenn R. "The Ethics of the *Wealth of Nations.*" *Philosophical Review* 34 (November 1925): 599–611.

455 Morrow, Glenn R. "The Significance of the Doctrine of Sympathy in Hume and Adam Smith." *Philosophical Review* 32 (March 1923): 60–78.

456 Prior, Elizabeth. "Smith on 'Distributions.' " *Australian Journal of Philosophy* 59 (June 1981): 206–10.

457 Radner, John B. "The Art of Sympathy in Eighteenth-century British Moral Thought." *Studies in Eighteenth-century Culture* 9 (1979): 189–210.

458 Scott, William R. "New Light on Adam Smith." *Economic Journal* 46 (September 1936): 401–11.

459 Shott, Susan. "Society, Self, and Mind in Moral Philosophy: The Scottish Moralists as Precursors of Symbolic Interactionism." *Journal of the History of the Behavioral Sciences* 12, no. 1 (1976): 39–46.

460 Skinner, Andrew S. "Adam Smith: The Development of a System." *Scottish Journal of Political Economy* 23 (June 1976): 111–51.

461 Taylor, Overton H. "Economics and the Idea of Ius Naturale." *Quarterly Journal of Economics* 44 (February 1930): 205–41.

462 West, Edwin G. "Adam Smith and Rousseau's *Discourse on Inequality:* Inspiration or Provocation?" *Journal of Economic Issues* 5 (June 1971): 56–70.

463 West, Edwin G. "Adam Smith's Philosophy of Riches." *Philosophy* 44 (April 1969): 101–15.

BOOKS

464 Arrowood, Charles F. *Theory of Education in the Political Philosophy of Adam Smith.* Austin, Tex.: Privately printed, 1945.

465 Bagolini, Luigi. "The Topicality of Adam Smith's Notion of Sympathy and Judicial Evaluations." In *Essays on Adam Smith,* edited by Andrew S. Skinner and Thomas Wilson, pp. 100–113. Oxford: Clarendon Press, 1975.

466 Bonar, James. "Adam Smith." In his *Moral Sense,* pp. 168–240. New York: Macmillan Co., 1930.

467 Buchanan, James M. "The Justice of Natural Liberty." In *Adam Smith and "The Wealth of Nations": 1776–1976,* edited by Fred R. Glahe, pp. 61–81. Boulder, Colo.: Colorado Associated University Press, 1978.

468 Cain, Roy E. "David Hume and Adam Smith: A Study in Intellectual Kinship." Ph.D. dissertation, University of Texas, 1963.

469 Campbell, Thomas. *Adam Smith's Science of Morals.* London: Allen & Unwin, 1971.

470 Campbell, Thomas. "Scientific Explanation and Ethical Justification in the *Moral Sentiments.*" In *Essays on Adam Smith,* edited by Andrew S. Skinner and Thomas Wilson, pp. 68–82. Oxford: Clarendon Press, 1975.

471 Campbell, William. "Prudence, Justice, and Beneficence." Ph.D. dissertation, University of Virginia, 1966.

472 Colletti, Lucio. "Mandeville, Rousseau, and Smith." In his *From Rousseau to Lenin: Studies in Ideology and Society,* translated by John Merrington and Judith White, pp. 195–216. New York: Monthly Review Press, 1973.

473 Cropsey, Joseph. "Adam Smith." In *History of Political Philosophy,* 2d ed., edited by Leo Strauss and Joseph Cropsey, pp. 607–30. Chicago: Rand McNally, 1972.

474 Cropsey, Joseph. "Adam Smith and Political Philosophy." In *Essays on Adam Smith,* edited by Andrew S. Skinner and Thomas Wilson, pp. 132–53. Oxford: Clarendon Press, 1975.

475 Cropsey, Joseph. *Polity and Economics: An Interpretation of the Principles of Adam Smith.* The Hague: Nijhoff, 1957. Reprint ed., Westport, Conn.: Greenwood Press, 1977.

476 Farrer, James A. *Adam Smith (1723–1790).* New York: Putnam; London: Low, 1881.

477 Jack, Henry H. "The Moral Philosophy of Adam Smith." Ph.D. dissertation, Harvard University, 1955.

478 Lightwood, Martha B. "Adam Smith: Moral Philosopher and Political Economist." Ph.D. dissertation, University of Pennsylvania, 1978.

479 McCosh, James. "Adam Smith, 1723–1790." In his *The Scottish Philosophy: Biographical, Expository, Critical, from Hutcheson to Hamilton,* pp. 162–73. New York: Robert Carter, 1875. Reprint ed., New York: AMS Press, 1980.

480 Macfie, Alec L. *The Individual in Society: Papers on Adam Smith.* University of Glasgow Social and Economic Studies, no. 11. London: Allen & Unwin, 1967.

481 Mizuti, Hiroshi. "Moral Philosophy and Civil Society." In *Essays on Adam Smith,* edited by Andrew S. Skinner and Thomas Wilson, pp. 114–31. Oxford: Clarendon Press, 1975.

482 Morrow, Glenn R. "Adam Smith: Moralist and Philosopher." In *Adam Smith, 1776–1926 . . . ,* by John M. Clark et al., pp. 156–79. Chicago: University of Chicago Press, 1928. Reprint ed., New York: Kelley, 1966.

483 Muir, Ethel. *The Ethical System of Adam Smith.* Halifax, Nova Scotia: Bowers, 1898.

484 Paul, Ellen Frankel. *Moral Revolution and Economic Science: The Demise of Laissez-faire in Nineteenth-century British Political Economy.* Contributions in Economics and Economic History, no. 23. Westport, Conn., and London: Greenwood Press, 1979.

485 Raphael, David D. "Adam Smith's Philosophy, Science, and Social Science." In *Philosophers of the Enlightenment,* edited by S. C. Brown, Royal Institute of Philosophers Lectures, vol. 12, pp. 77–93. Brighton, Eng.: Harvester Press, 1979.

486 Raphael, David D. *The Impartial Spectator.* Dawes Hicks Lecture on Philosophy, 1972. London: Oxford University Press, 1973.

487 Raphael, David D. "The Impartial Spectator." In *Essays on Adam Smith,* edited by Andrew S. Skinner and Thomas Wilson, pp. 83–99. Oxford: Clarendon Press, 1975.

488   Robbins, Caroline. "Francis Hutcheson and Adam Smith." In her *The Eighteenth-century Commonwealthman*, pp. 185–99. Cambridge, Mass.: Harvard University Press, 1959.

489   Schneider, Herbert L., ed. *Adam Smith's Moral and Political Philosophy.* New York: Hafner, 1948. Reprint ed., New York: Harper Torchbooks, 1970.

490   Schneider, Louis, ed. *The Scottish Moralists on Human Nature and Society.* Chicago: University of Chicago Press, 1967. (Various comments on Smith's moral philosophy and theory of society are found chiefly on pp. xxix–xli and lxii–lxv.)

491   Selby-Bigge, Louis. *British Moralists.* Vol. 1. Oxford: Clarendon Press, 1897. (Comments on Adam Smith are on pp. 255–336.)

492   Skinner, Andrew S. "Adam Smith: Science and the Role of the Imagination." In *Hume and the Enlightenment: Essays Presented to Ernest Campbell Mossner,* edited by William B. Todd, pp. 164–88. Austin: University of Texas, Humanities Research Center; Edinburgh: University Press, 1974.

493   Sowell, Thomas. "Adam Smith in Theory and Practice." In *Adam Smith and "The Wealth of Nations": 1776–1976,* edited by Fred R. Glahe, pp. 148–72. Boulder, Colo.: Colorado Associated University Press, 1978.

494   Swabey, William C. "Adam Smith." In his *Ethical Theory: From Hobbes to Kant,* pp. 178–97. New York: Philosophical Library, 1961.

495   Tsanoff, Radoslav A. "Ethics of Sympathy." In his *The Moral Ideals of Our Civilization,* pp. 274–89. New York: Dutton, 1942.

496   Wilson, Thomas. "Sympathy and Self-interest." In *The Market and the State: Essays in Honour of Adam Smith,* edited by Thomas Wilson and Andrew S. Skinner, pp. 73–99 (followed by comments by R. S. Downie and Mancur Olson, pp. 99–112). Oxford: Clarendon Press, 1976.

Social Theory

ARTICLES

497   Becker, James F. "Adam Smith's Theory of Social Science." *Southern Economic Journal* 28 (July 1961): 13–21.

498   Bryson, Gladys. "Some Eighteenth-century Conceptions of Society." *Sociological Review* 31 (October 1939): 401–21.

499 Camic, Charles. "Utilitarians Revisited." *American Journal of Sociology* 85 (November 1979): 516–50. "Discussion," *American Journal of Sociology* 86 (March 1981): 1133–44.

500 Coats, Alfred W. "Adam Smith: The Modern Re-appraisal." *Renaissance and Modern Studies* 6 (1962): 25–48.

501 Cumming, Robert D. "Giving Back Words: Things, Money, Persons." *Social Research* 48, no. 2 (1981): 227–59.

502 Jones, Robert A. "On Camic's Antipresentist Methodology." *American Journal of Sociology* 86, no. 5 (1981): 1133–44.

503 Lamb, Robert B. "Adam Smith's System: Sympathy Not Self-interest." *Journal of the History of Ideas* 35 (October–December 1974): 671–82.

504 Mayer, Joseph. "Perfect Man, Perfect Competition, and the Spoils of War." *Social Science* 39 (January 1964): 3–14.

505 Salomen, Albert. "Adam Smith as Sociologist." *Social Research* 12 (February 1945): 22–42.

506 Spiegel, Henry W. "Adam Smith's Heavenly City." *History of Political Economy* 8 (Winter 1976): 478–93.

507 Swengelwood, Alan. "Origins of Sociology: The Case of the Scottish Enlightenment." *British Journal of Sociology* 21 no. 2 (1970): 164–80.

508 Worland, Stephen T. "Philosophy, Welfare, and 'The System of Natural Liberty'." *Review of Social Economy* 11 (September 1963): 117–30.

BOOKS

509 Danner, Peter L. "An Inquiry into the Social Aspects of Adam Smith's Theory of Value." Ph.D. dissertation, Syracuse University, 1964.

510 Ellwood, C. A. "Later Eighteenth-century British Social Philosophy." In his *Story of Social Philosophy*, pp. 252–69. New York: Prentice-Hall, 1938.

511 Foley, Vernard. *The Social Physics of Adam Smith*. West Lafayette, Ind.: Purdue University Press, 1976.

512 Lindgren, J. Ralph. *The Social Philosophy of Adam Smith*. The Hague: Nijhoff, 1973.

513 Patten, Simon N. *The Development of English Thought: A Study in*

the *Economic Interpretation of History.* New York and London: Macmillan, 1899. Pp. 50–56, 226–43.

514 Skinner, Andrew S. *A System of Social Science: Papers Relating to Adam Smith.* Oxford: Clarendon Press, 1979.

515 Small, Albion W. *Adam Smith and Modern Sociology: A Study in the Methodology of the Social Sciences.* Chicago: University of Chicago Press; London: Unwin, 1907.

516 Spengler, Joseph J. "Adam Smith and Society's Decision-makers." In *Essays on Adam Smith,* edited by Andrew S. Skinner and Thomas Wilson, pp. 390–414. Oxford: Clarendon Press, 1975.

517 Strong, Gordon. *Adam Smith and the Eighteenth Century Concept of Social Progress.* St. Louis, Mo.: Eden Publishing House, 1932.

518 Strong, Gordon. "Adam Smith and the Eighteenth Century Concept of Social Progress." Ph.D. dissertation, University of Chicago, 1932.

Society and the Economy

ARTICLES

519 Becker, James F. "The Corporation Spirit and Its Liberal Analysis." *Journal of the History of Ideas* 30 (January 1969): 69–84.

520 Coats, Alfred W. "Adam Smith's Conception of Self-interest in Economic and Political Affairs." *History of Political Economy* 7 (Spring 1975): 132–36.

521 Connolly, John M. "Adam Smith on Wealth and Authority." *Philosophy Research Archives* 4 (1978).

522 Danford, John W. "Adam Smith, Equality, and the Wealth of Sympathy." *American Journal of Political Science* 24 (November 1980): 674–95.

523 Gramm, Warren S. "The Selective Interpretation of Adam Smith." *Journal of Economic Issues* 14 (March 1980): 119–42.

524 Heinrich, B. "The Invisible Hand Loses Its Grip." *Business and Society Review* 12 (Winter 1974–75): 30–34.

525 Merrill, B. "Adam Smith's Commercial Society as a Surrogate for Morals." *Economic Forum* 12 (Summer 1981): 65–74.

526 Miller, S. "Adam Smith and the Commercial Republic." *Public Interest* 61 (Fall 1980): 106–22.

527 Nord, Walter. "Adam Smith and the Contemporary Social Exchange

Theory." *American Journal of Economics and Sociology* 32 (October 1973): 421–36.

528 Powers, Richard H. "Adam Smith, Practical Realist." *Southwestern Social Science Quarterly* 37 (December 1956): 222–33.

529 Rosenberg, Nathan. "Adam Smith, Consumer Tastes, and Economic Growth." *Journal of Political Economy* 76 (May–June 1968): 361–74.

530 Samuels, Warren J. "Adam Smith and the Economy as a System of Power." *Indian Economic Journal* 20 (January–March 1973): 363–81.

531 Samuels, Warren J. "Adam Smith and the Economy as a System of Power." *Review of Social Economy* 31 (October 1973): 123–37.

532 Samuels, Warren J. "The Classical Theory of Economic Policy: Nonlegal Social Controls, Part I." *Southern Economic Journal* 31 (July 1964): 1–20.

533 Samuels, Warren J. "The Classical Theory of Economic Policy: Nonlegal Social Controls, Part II." *Southern Economic Journal* 31 (October 1964): 87–100.

534 Skinner, Andrew S. "Natural History in the Age of Adam Smith." *Political Studies* 15 (February 1967): 32–48.

535 Sobel, Irvin. "Adam Smith: What Kind of Institutionalist Was He?" *Journal of Economic Issues* 13 (June 1979): 347–68.

BOOKS

536 Fischer, Norman. *Economy and Self: Philosophy and Economics, from the Mercantilists to Marx.* Contributions in Economics and Economic History, no. 24. Westport, Conn., and London: Greenwood Press, 1979.

537 Heilbroner, Robert L. "The Wonderful World of Adam Smith." In his *The Worldly Philosophers,* pp. 26–57. New York: Simon & Schuster, 1953.

538 Reisman, David A. *Adam Smith's Sociological Economics.* New York: Harper & Row; London: Croom Helm, 1976.

539 Robbins, Lionel. *The Theory of Economic Policy in English Classical Political Economy.* 2d ed. Philadelphia: Porcupine Press, [1952], 1978.

540 Skinner, Andrew S. "Adam Smith: An Economic Interpretation of History." In *Essays on Adam Smith,* edited by Andrew S. Skinner

and Thomas Wilson, pp. 154–78. Oxford: Clarendon Press, 1975.
541 Sobel, Irvin. *Adam Smith's Solicitude for the Poor and Skepticism About the Wealthy.* Richmond, Va.: Eastern Kentucky University Press, 1977.
542 Sowell, Thomas. *Classical Economics Reconsidered.* Princeton: Princeton University Press, 1974. (Analyses of the social philosophy of Adam Smith and others.)

Morality, Society, and the Individual

ARTICLES

543 Baumol, William J. "Smith vs. Marx on Business Morality and the Social Interest." *American Economist* 20 (Fall 1976): 1–6.
544 Campbell, T. D., and Ross, Ian S. "Utilitarianism of Adam Smith's Policy Advice." *Journal of the History of Ideas* 42 (January–March 1981): 73–92.
545 Davenport, Herbert. "The Ethics of the *Wealth of Nations.*" *Philosophical Review* 34 (November 1925): 599–609.
546 De Grood, David H. "The New Era: 'Homo Oeconomicus.'" *Revolutionary World* 16 (Special issue, 1976): 4–20.
547 Heilbroner, Robert L. "Socialization of the Individual in Adam Smith." *History of Political Economy* 14 (Fall 1982): 426–39.
548 Laird, John. "The Social Philosophy of Smith's *Wealth of Nations.*" *Journal of Philosophic Studies* 2 (January 1927): 39–51.
549 Petrella, Frank. "Individual, Group, or Government? Smith, Mill, and Sidgwick." *History of Political Economy* 2 (Spring 1970): 152–76.
550 Rimlinger, Gaston V. "Smith and the Merits of the Poor." *Review of Social Economy* 34 (December 1976): 333–44.
551 Rohrlich, George F. "The Role of Self-interest in the Social Economy of Life, Liberty, and the Pursuit of Happiness, *Anno* 1976 and Beyond." *Review of Social Economy* 34, no. 3 (1976): 373–78.

BOOKS

552 Billet, Leonard. "Justice, Liberty, and Economy." In *Adam Smith and "The Wealth of Nations": 1776–1976,* edited by Fred R. Glahe, pp. 83–109. Boulder, Colo.: Colorado Associated University Press, 1978.

553 Tufts, James H. "The Individual and the Creation of Social Forces—Adam Smith." In his *The Individual and His Relation to Society, as Reflected in the British Ethics of the Eighteenth Century*, pp. 47–58. University of Chicago Contributions to Philosophy, vol. 1, no. 6. New York: Macmillan Co., 1904. Reprint ed., New York: Kelley, 1970.

The Relationship of *Theory of Moral Sentiments* to *Wealth of Nations*

ARTICLES

554 Bitterman, Henry J. "Adam Smith's Empiricism and the Law of Nature, I." *Journal of Political Economy* 48 (August 1940): 487–520.

555 Bitterman, Henry J. "Adam Smith's Empiricism and the Law of Nature, II." *Journal of Political Economy* 48 (October 1940): 703–34.

556 Coats, Alfred W. "Political Affairs." *History of Political Economy* 7 (March 1975): 132–36.

557 Macfie, Alec. "Adam Smith's *Moral Sentiments* as Foundation for His *Wealth of Nations*." *Oxford Economic Papers*, n.s., 11 (October 1959): 209–28.

558 Oncken, August. "The Consistency of Adam Smith." *Economic Journal* 7 (September 1897): 443–50.

559 Stein, Peter. "Adam Smith's Jurisprudence: Between Morality and Economics." *Cornell Law Review* 64 (April 1979): 621–38.

560 Teichgraeber, Richard. "Rethinking das Adam Smith Problem." *Journal of British Studies* 20 (Spring 1981): 106–23.

561 Venning, Corey. "The World of Adam Smith Revisited." *Studies in Burke and His Time* 19, no. 1 (1978): 61–71.

BOOKS

562 Buckle, Henry T. *History of Civilization in England*. 2 vols. New York: Appleton, 1903. (Commentary on Smith is in vol. 2, chap. 6, pp. 340–57.)

563 Morrow, Glenn R. *The Ethical and Economic Theories of Adam*

Smith. Cornell Studies in Philosophy, no. 13. New York: Long-mans, 1923. Reprint ed., New York: Kelley, 1969.

564 Scott, William R. "Adam Smith." In *Proceedings of the British Academy,* vol. 10, 1921–23, pp. 435–53. [Paper read June 6, 1923.] London: The Academy, 1924.

Government, Politics, and Law

ARTICLES

565 Ayres, Clarence E. "The *Wealth of Nations.*" *Southwestern Social Science Quarterly* 21 (June 1940): 1–9.

566 Bastable, Charles F. "Adam Smith's Lectures on Jurisprudence." *Hermathena* 10 (1889): 200–211.

567 Billet, Leonard. "Political Order and Economic Development: Reflections on Adam Smith's *Wealth of Nations.*" *Political Studies* 23 (December 1975): 430–41.

568 Campbell, Thomas D. "Adam Smith and Natural Liberty." *Political Studies* 25 (December 1977): 523–34.

569 Cooke, C. A. "Adam Smith and Jurisprudence." *Law Quarterly Review* 51 (April 1935): 326–32.

570 Devine, Donald J. "Adam Smith and the Problem of Justice in Capitalist Society." *Journal of Legal Studies* 6 (June 1977): 399–410.

571 Eliot, Thomas D. "The Relations Between Adam Smith and Benjamin Franklin." *Political Science Quarterly* 39 (March 1924): 67–96.

572 Forbes, Duncan. "Scientific Whiggism, Adam Smith, and John Millar." *Cambridge Journal* 7 (August 1954): 643–70.

573 Freeman, R. D. "Adam Smith, Education, and Laissez-faire." *History of Political Economy* 1 (Spring 1969): 173–86.

574 Gay, David E. R. "Adam Smith and Property Rights Analysis." *Review of Social Economy* 33 (October 1975): 177–79.

575 Glenn, Gary D. "Inalienable Rights and Positive Government in the Modern World." *Journal of Politics* 41, no. 4 (1979): 1057–80.

576 Grampp, William D. "On the Politics of the Classical Economists." *Quarterly Journal of Economics* 62 (November 1948): 714–47.

577 Hasbach, Wilhelm. "Adam Smith's Lectures on Justice, Police, Revenue, and Arms." *Political Science Quarterly* 12 (October 1897): 684–98.

578   Sorzano, J. S. "David Easton and the Invisible Hand." *American Political Science Review* 69 (March 1975): 91–106.
579   Spengler, Joseph J. "Adam Smith on Human Capital." *American Economic Review* 67 (February 1977): 32–36.
580   Stigler, George J. "Smith's Travels on the Ship of State." *History of Political Economy* 3 (Fall 1971): 265–77.
581   West, Edwin G. "Adam Smith's Public Economics." *Canadian Journal of Economics* 10 (February 1977): 1–18.

BOOKS

582   Buchanan, James M. "Public Goods and Natural Liberty." In *The Market and the State: Essays in Honour of Adam Smith,* edited by Thomas Wilson and Andrew S. Skinner, pp. 271–86 (followed by comments by E. J. Mishan and Alan Williams, pp. 286–95). Oxford: Clarendon Press, 1976.
583   Cannan, Edwin. "Editor's Introduction: History of the Report, Value of the Report, Table of Parallel Passages in *The Wealth of Nations.*" In his *Lectures on Justice, Police, Revenue, and Arms, by Adam Smith,* pp. xi–xxxv. Oxford: Clarendon Press, 1896.
584   Forbes, Duncan. "Skeptical Whiggism, Commerce, and Liberty." In *Essays on Adam Smith,* edited by Andrew S. Skinner and Thomas Wilson, pp. 179–201. Oxford: Clarendon Press, 1975.
585   Haakonssen, Knud. *The Science of a Legislator: The Natural Jurisprudence of David Hume and Adam Smith.* Cambridge: Cambridge University Press, 1981.
586   Raphael, David D. "Hume and Adam Smith on Justice and Utility." In *Proceedings of the Aristotelian Society,* pp. 87–103. London: Methuen, 1973.
587   Reisman, David A. *Tawney, Galbraith, and Adam Smith; State and Welfare.* New York: St. Martin's, 1982.
588   Skinner, Andrew S. *Adam Smith and the Role of the State: A Paper Delivered in Kircaldy on 5 June 1973 at a Symposium to Commemorate the 250th Anniversary of the Birth of Adam Smith.* Glasgow: University of Glasgow Press, 1974.
589   Skinner, Andrew S. "Adam Smith: The Origin, Nature, and the Function of Government." Glasgow: University of Glasgow, [1975].

590 Stigler, George J. "Smith's Travels on the Ship of State." In *Essays on Adam Smith*, edited by Andrew S. Skinner and Thomas Wilson, pp. 237–46. Oxford: Clarendon Press, 1975.

591 Tronto, Joan C. "Is Political Rationality Possible? A Critique of Political Control in the Work of Hobbes, Smith, and Weber." Ph.D. dissertation, Princeton University, 1981.

592 Unger, James A. "The Ascendancy of Society: Adam Smith and the Apolitical Vision of the Augustan Age." Ph.D. dissertation, State University of New York at Albany, 1973.

593 Winch, Donald. *Adam Smith's Politics: An Essay in Historiographic Revision*. Cambridge Studies in the History and Theory of Politics. New York, London, and Melbourne: Cambridge University Press, 1978.

594 Youngson, Alexander J. *Adam Smith and the Omnipresent State*. Newcastle, Australia: University of Newcastle, Department of Economics, 1976.

The Colonies and the American Revolution

ARTICLES

595 "Adam Smith as Imperialist." *Saturday Review* 99 (January 7, 1905): 19–20.

596 Benians, Ernest A. "Adam Smith's Project of an Empire." *Cambridge Historical Journal* 1, no. 1 (1925): 249–83.

597 Fagerstrom, Dalphy I. "Scottish Opinion and the American Revolution." *William and Mary Quarterly* 11 (April 1954): 253–75.

598 Fay, Charles R. "Adam Smith, America, and the Doctrinal Defeat of the Mercantile System." *Quarterly Journal of Economics* 48 (February 1934): 304–16.

599 Grampp, William D. "Adam Smith and the American Revolutionists." *History of Political Economy* 11 (Summer 1979): 179–91.

600 Kittrell, Edward. "The Development of the Theory of Colonization in English Classical Political Economy." *Southern Economic Journal* 31 (January 1965): 189–206.

601 Leslie, Thomas Edward Cliffe. "*The Wealth of Nations* and the Slave Trade." *Macmillan's Magazine* 7 (February 1863): 269–76.

602 Nicholson, Joseph S. "The Economics of Imperialism." *Economic Journal* 20 (June 1910): 155–71.

603 Skinner, Andrew S. "Adam Smith and the American Economic Community: An Essay in Applied Economics." *Journal of the History of Ideas* 37 (January–March 1976): 59–78.

BOOKS

604 Clark, John M. "Adam Smith and the Spirit of '76." In *The Spirit of '76 and Other Essays*, edited by Carl Becker et al., pp. 61–98. Washington, D.C.: Robert Brookings Graduate School, 1928.

605 Ghosh, R. N. "Adam Smith and His Contemporaries." In his *Classical Macro-economics and the Case for Colonies*. Calcutta: New Age Publishers, 1967(?).

606 Koebner, Richard. *Empire*. Cambridge: Cambridge University Press, 1961.

607 Stevens, David. "Adam Smith and the Colonial Disturbances." In *Essays on Adam Smith*, edited by Andrew S. Skinner and Thomas Wilson, pp. 202–17. Oxford: Clarendon Press, 1975.

608 Winch, Donald. *Classical Political Economy and Colonies*. Cambridge, Mass.: Harvard University Press, 1965. (See especially chap. 2.)

Miscellaneous Works

ARTICLES

609 Baudet, H. "Adam Smith and Glasgow, Accompanying the New Glasgow Edition of the *Wealth of Nations*." *De Economía* 124, no. 4 (1976): 395–402.

610 Berry, Christopher J. "Adam Smith's 'Considerations' on Language." *Journal of the History of Ideas* 35 (January–March 1974): 130–38.

611 Bevilacqua, Vincent M. "Adam Smith and Some Philosophical Origins of Eighteenth-century Rhetorical Theory." *Modern Language Review* 43 (July 1968): 559–68.

612 Bevilacqua, Vincent M. "Adam Smith's *Lectures on Rhetoric and*

Belles Lettres." *Studies in Scottish Literature* 3 (July 1965/66): 41–59.

613 Bodkin, Ronald G. "A Retrospective Look at Adam Smith's Views on University Education." *Eastern Economic Journal* 3 (April 1976): 64–71.

614 Bryce, J. C. "Literary Views of Adam Smith." *Notes and Queries* 20 (November 1973): 423.

615 Cole, Arthur. "Puzzles of the *Wealth of Nations.*" *Canadian Journal of Economics and Political Science* 24 (February 1958): 1–8. (Paradoxes in Smith's opinions of merchants, farmers, politicians, bankers, etc.)

616 "[Conversation between] Adam Smith and Highland Laird." *Blackwood's Magazine* 3 (July 1818): 419–20. (Humorous short essay.)

617 Davis, Joseph A. "Adam Smith and the Human Stomach." *Quarterly Journal of Economics* 68 (May 1954): 275–86.

618 Dow, Louis A. "The Rise of the City: Adam Smith Versus Henri Pirenne." *Review of Social Economy* 32 (October 1974): 170–85.

619 Grandjean, Burke D. "The Division of Labor, Technology, and Education: Cross-national Evidence." *Social Science Quarterly* 55, no. 2 (1974): 297–309.

620 Grigg, David. "Sir James Steuart and Land Use Theory: A Note." *Scottish Geographical Magazine* 95, no. 2 (1979): 108–10.

621 Heilbroner, Robert L. "The Paradox of Progress: Decline and Decay in the *Wealth of Nations.*" *Journal of the History of Ideas* 34 (April 1973): 243–62.

622 Kilborn, Peter B. "Adam Smith Recognized Anew." *New York Times*, April 6, 1976, p. 47+. (Lengthy article on the bicentennial meeting at Glasgow.)

623 Lackman, Conway L. "The Modern Development of Classical Rent Theory." *American Journal of Economics and Sociology* 36, no. 1 (1977): 51–64.

624 Land, Stephen K. "Adam Smith's 'Considerations Concerning the First Formation of Languages.'" *Journal of the History of Ideas* 38 (October–December 1977): 677–90.

625 Lee, Joseph. "Adam Smith on the Need for Community Service: Quotations from *Wealth of Nations.*" *Playground* 14 (July 1920): 215–18.

626 Levy, David. "Marcuse, Metaphysics, and Marxism." *Philosophy Today* 23 (Summer 1979): 128–37.

627 Malek, James S. "Adam Smith's Contribution to Eighteenth-century

British Aesthetics." *Journal of Aesthetics and Art Criticism* 31 (Fall 1972): 49–54.

628 Miller, William L. "Primogeniture, Entails, and Endowments in English Economics." *History of Political Economy* 12, no. 4 (1980): 558–81.

629 Phillips, J. D. "The Theory of Small Enterprise: Smith, Mill, Marshall, and Marx." *Explorations in Economic History* 16 (July 1979): 331–40.

630 Romanos, John H. "[Communication Relating to the Muir Portrait of Adam Smith.]" *Economic Journal* 55 (December 1945): 465–66.

631 Rothschild, Lincoln. "Further Thoughts on the Aesthetics of Adam Smith." *Journal of Aesthetics and Art Criticism* 31 (Summer 1973): 541–42.

632 Watson, J. Wreford. "Land Use and Adam Smith: A Bicentennial Note." *Scottish Geographical Magazine* 92, no. 2 (1976): 129–34.

633 Weaver, J. J., and Wisman, J. D. "Smith, Marx, and Malthus." *Futurist* 12 (April 1978): 92–94+.

634 Worland, Stephen T. "Mechanistic Analogy and Smith on Exchange." *Review of Social Economy* 34 (December 1976): 245–58.

BOOKS

635 *The Adam Smith Centennial to Commemorate the Hundredth Anniversary of the Publication of the "Wealth of Nations."* New York: New Century, 1876. (Reprinted from *New Century,* no. 10, 1876.)

636 Adam Smith Club, Glasgow. *The Adam Smith Club, Glasgow, 1868–97.* Glasgow: The Club, 1897(?). (Historical sketch of the Club; Roll of Members, 1897; Record of Subjects Discussed by the Club.)

637 Adam Smith Club, London. . . . *Rules, By-laws, and Members.* London(?): The Club, 1855.

638 Alchian, A. "On Corporations: A Visit with Smith." Los Angeles: Foundation for Research in Economics and Education, 1976.

639 Blaug, Mark. "The Economics of Education in English Classical Political Economy. A Re-examination." In *Essays on Adam Smith,* ed-

ited by Andrew S. Skinner and Thomas Wilson, pp. 568–99. Oxford: Clarendon Press, 1975.

640 Bonar, James. *The Tables Turned*. London: Macmillan & Co., 1931. Reprint ed., New York: Kelley, 1970.

641 Cunningham, William. *Back to Adam Smith*. Read to the Scottish Society of Economists on December 15, 1903. Edinburgh: Blackwood & Sons, 1904.

642 Feingold, Richard. "Bucolic Tradition and Virtuous Work: Arthur Young and Adam Smith." In his *Nature and Society: Later Eighteenth-century Uses of the Pastoral and Gregoric*, pp. 51–82. New Brunswick, N.J.: Rutgers University Press, 1978.

643 Heilbroner, Robert L. "The Paradox of Progress: Decline and Decay in *The Wealth of the Nations*." In *Essays on Adam Smith*, edited by Andrew S. Skinner and Thomas Wilson, pp. 524–39. Oxford: Clarendon Press, 1975.

644 Howell, Wilbur S. "Adam Smith's 'Lectures on Rhetoric': An Historical Assessment." In *Essays on Adam Smith*, edited by Andrew S. Skinner and Thomas Wilson, pp. 11–43. Oxford: Clarendon Press, 1975.

645 Howell, Wilbur S. *Eighteenth-century British Logic and Rhetoric*. Princeton: Princeton University Press, 1977. (Various comments on *Early Writings* and *Theory of Moral Sentiments*.)

646 Hume, David. *The Letters of David Hume*. 2 vols. Edited by John Y. T. Greig. Oxford: Clarendon Press, 1932. (Includes letters from Hume to Smith.)

647 MacLean, Kenneth. "Agrarian Economists: The Physiocrats and Adam Smith." In his *The Agrarian Age: A Background for Wordsworth*, pp. 65–80. Yale Studies in English, vol. 115. New Haven: Yale University Press, 1950.

648 Malek, James S. "Adam Smith's Analysis of the Imitative Arts and Instrumental Music." In his *The Arts Compared: An Aspect of Eighteenth-century British Aesthetics*. Detroit: Wayne State University Press, 1974.

649 Malthus, Thomas R. "On the Definition and Application of Terms by Adam Smith." In his *Definitions in Political Economy*, pp. 10–18. London: Murray, 1827.

650 Morgan, Frank. "Adam Smith and Belles Lettres: An Attempt to Establish the Philosophical Basis and to Formulate the Central Tenets of His Belletristic Thought." Ph.D. dissertation, University of Mississippi, 1966.

651 Pike, Edgar R. *Human Documents of Adam Smith's Time*. London:

Allen & Unwin, 1974. (Excerpts from journals, accounts of travelers, and descriptive books written in the eighteenth century about social conditions in England and Scotland which illustrate Smith's views on society. See especially "Adam Smith: The Man and His Book," pp. 17–25.)

652   Scott, William R. "Adam Smith and the City of Glasgow." In *Proceedings of the Royal Philosophical Society of Glasgow*, vol. 52, 1923, pp. 138–48. Glasgow: The Society, 1924.

653   Trivoli, George W. *The Suffolk Bank*. London: Adam Smith Institute, 1979.

654   Watson, J. Wreford. "Adam Smith, *Wealth of Nations*, and Edinburgh New Town." In *Transactions of the Royal Society of Canada*, series 4, vol. 14, 1976, pp. 241–54.

655   Wilson, Thomas. "Some Concluding Reflections." In *Essays on Adam Smith*, edited by Andrew S. Skinner and Thomas Wilson, pp. 600–612. Oxford: Clarendon Press, 1975.

Collections of Readings

ARTICLES

656   Waters, W. R., ed. "Social Economics of Adam Smith [symposium]." *Review of Social Economy* 34 (December 1976): 239–390.

657   "*Wealth of Nations* Bicentenary: A Symposium." *Scottish Journal of Political Economy* 23 (June 1976): 109–203.

BOOKS

658   *Adam Smith and Modern Political Economy: Bicentennial Essays on "The Wealth of Nations."* Edited by Gerald P. O'Driscoll, Jr. Ames: Iowa State University Press, 1979.

659   *Adam Smith and the "Wealth of Nations," 1776–1976.* Edited and with an introduction by Fred R. Glahe. Boulder, Colo.: Colorado Associated University Press, 1978.

660   *Adam Smith, 1776–1926 . . .* by John M. Clark et al. Chicago: University of Chicago Press, 1928. Reprint ed., New York: Kelley, 1966.

661 *Adam Smith, 1723–1973: Commemorative Symposium,* Kircaldy, Scotland, June 5 and 6, 1973. Kircaldy, Scotland: Kircaldy Town Council, 1974. (Speeches by Arthur Burns, the Right Hon. Lord O'Brian, Andrew Skinner, Sir John Toohill, Hiroshi Mizuti, and John K. Galbraith.)

662 Bradley, Ian, and Howard, Michael, eds. *Classical and Marxian Political Economy: Essays in Honor of Ronald L. Meek.* New York: St. Martin's, 1982.

663 Fay, Charles R. *The World of Adam Smith.* Cambridge: W. Heffer, 1960.

664 *The Market and the State: Essays in Honour of Adam Smith.* Edited by Thomas Wilson and Andrew S. Skinner. Oxford: Clarendon Press, 1976.

665 Napoleoni, Claudio. *Smith, Ricardo, Marx.* New York: Wiley, 1975. (Translation of the 2d Italian edition by G. M. S. Gee. Reprints of articles.)

666 Political Economy Club. *Political Economy Club . . . Revised Report of the Proceedings at the Dinner of 31st May 1876. Held in Celebration of the Hundredth Year of the Publication of the "Wealth of Nations."* London: Longmans, 1876.

667 Skinner, Andrew S., and Wilson, Thomas, eds. *Essays on Adam Smith.* Clarendon: Oxford University Press, 1975.

Brief Commentaries

ARTICLES

668 Chalk, Alfred F. "Natural Law and the Rise of Economic Individualism in England." *Journal of Political Economy* 59 (August 1951): 332–47. (References to Smith are included.)

669 "The Commemoration of Adam Smith at Glasgow," by W. R. S. [William R. Scott]. *Economic Journal* 48 (September 1938): 571.

670 De Grood, David H. "The New Era: The Rosy Dawn and Revolutionary Theory." *Revolutionary World* 16 (Special issue 1976): 1–3.

671 Galbraith, John K. "The Language of Economists." *Fortune* 66 (December 1962): 128. (Subheading: "That Lively Stylist, Adam Smith.")

672 Grossman, H. "The Evolutionist Revolt Against Classical Economics."

Journal of Political Economy 51 (October 1943): 381–96. (Smith is mentioned on pp. 384–85.)

673 Heilbroner, Robert L. "The Adam Smith Nobody Knows." *Journal of Portfolio Management* 2 (Summer 1976): 65–66.

674 Holtrop, M. W. "Theories of the Velocity of Circulation of Money in Earlier Economic Literature." *Economic History* (supplement to *Economic Journal*) 1 (January 1929): 503–24. (Smith especially on pp. 513–14.)

675 Jackson, J. "A Note on Adam Smith's Second Regulator of Wealth." *Economic Affairs* 25 (January–March 1980): 28–30.

676 Jackson, J. "A Note on Adam Smith's Second Regulator of Wealth." *Indian Economic Journal* 28 (January–March 1982): 105–6.

677 Jensen, Hans E. "Economics as Social Economics: The Views of the 'Founding Fathers.'" *Review of Social Economics* 35, no. 3 (1977): 239–58.

678 Moos, S. "Laissez-faire, Planning, and Ethics." *Economic Journal* 55 (April 1945): 17–27. (Brief mention of Adam Smith.)

679 O'Connor, John. "Smith and Marshall on the Individual's Supply of Labor: A Note." *International Labor Relations Review* 14 (January 1961): 273–76.

680 Samuelson, Paul A. "Economists and the History of Ideas." *American Economic Review* 52 (March 1962): 1–18. (Comments on Smith are on pp. 7 and 8.)

681 Sowell, Thomas. "Adam Smith's Shot Heard Round the World." *Fortune* 93 (March 1976): 179–80.

682 Van Den Haag, Ernest. "Haggis and the *Wealth of Nations*." *National Review* 29 (March 4, 1977): 268.

683 Viner, Jacob. "The Intellectual History of Laissez-faire." *Journal of Law and Economics* 3 (October 1960): 45–69. (Smith is discussed on pp. 59–60.)

BOOKS

684 Barber, William J. *A History of Economic Thought*. New York: Penguin, [1967], 1977. (Various references to Smith.)

685 Bogardus, Emory. "Individualistic Social Thought." In his *Development of Social Thought*, 2d ed., pp. 210–13. New York: Longmans, Green, 1947.

686 Bryson, Gladys. *Man and Society: The Scottish Inquiry of the Eight-*

eenth Century. Princeton: Princeton University Press, 1945. Reprint ed., New York: Kelley, 1968. (Scattered references to Adam Smith.)

687 Canterbery, E. Ray. *The Making of Economics.* Belmont, Calif.: Wadsworth, 1976. (Brief mention of Smith's inductive method.)

688 Dumont, Louis. *From Mandeville to Marx: The Genesis and Triumph of Economic Ideology.* Chicago: University of Chicago Press, 1977. (Various comments on Smith's economic analysis and philosophy.)

689 Flubacher, Joseph F. *The Concept of Ethics in the History of Economics.* New York: Vantage, 1950.

690 Friedman, Milton. "The Invisible Hand." In *The Business System: A Bicentennial View,* by Milton Friedman . . . [et al.] with an introduction by Frederick E. Webster, Jr., pp. 2–13. Hanover, N.H.: Amos Tuck School of Business Administration, distributed by the University Press of New England, 1977.

691 Galbraith, John K. *The Age of Uncertainty.* London: British Broadcasting Co. and André Deutsch, 1977. (Includes "The Prophets and Promise of Classical Capitalism: The Founder.")

692 Ghiselin, Michael T. *The Economy of Nature and the Evolution of Sex.* Berkeley: University of California Press, 1977. (Smith's theory that moral rules have adaptive significance is discussed.)

693 Grampp, William D. *Economic Liberalism.* New York: Random House, 1965. (Includes many short references to Adam Smith's thought.)

694 Gruchy, Allan. *Modern Economic Thought: The American Tradition.* New York: Prentice-Hall, 1947. (Comments on Smith's holistic approach.)

695 Honour, Frances M. *The State of the Industrial Revolution in 1776.* New York: Vantage Press, 1977.

696 Knight, Frank H. *On the History and Method of Economics: Selected Essays.* Chicago: University of Chicago Press, 1956.

697 Lekachman, Robert. *A History of Economic Ideas.* New York: McGraw-Hill, 1976. (Smith is discussed in section 2.)

698 Marx, Karl. *A Contribution to the Critique of Political Economy.* Edited and with an introduction by Maurice Dobb. New York: International Publishers, 1970. (Translation of *Zur Kritik der Politschen Ökonomie.* Scattered references to Smith's economic theories.)

699 Patten, Simon N. *Essays in Economic Theory.* New York: Knopf, 1924.

700 Randall, John H. "The Science of Man—The Sciences of Human

Nature and of Business." In his *The Making of the Modern Mind: A Survey of the Intellectual Background of the Present Age*, rev. ed., pp. 308–86. Boston: Houghton Mifflin, 1940. (Included in this section is a concise commentary on Adam Smith and commerce.)

701 Ricardo, David. *On the Principles of Political Economy and Taxation.* London: Murray, 1817. (Brief observations throughout on all aspects of Smith's economic theory.)

702 Robbins, Lionel. "Hume and Adam Smith." In his *The Theory of Economic Policy in English Classical Political Economy*, 2d ed., pp. 112–16. Philadelphia: Porcupine Press, 1978.

703 Robinson, Joan. *Economic Philosophy.* Chicago: Aldine, 1962.

704 Russell, Phillips. "Enter an Economist." In his *Glittering Century*, pp. 241–47. New York: Scribner's, 1936.

705 Samuels, Warren J. *The Classical Theory of Economic Policy.* Cleveland: World Publishing, 1966. (Comments on Smith are within pp. 25–40.)

706 Schumpeter, Joseph A. *History of Economic Analysis.* New York: Oxford University Press, 1954.

707 Stigler, George J. "The Politics of Political Economists." In his *Essays in the History of Economics*, pp. 67–70. Chicago: University of Chicago Press, 1965.

708 Viner, Jacob. *The Intellectual History of Laissez-faire.* The Henry Simons Lecture. Chicago: University of Chicago Law School, 1961.

709 Viner, Jacob. *Studies in the Theory of International Trade.* New York, London: Harper, 1937. (Brief references to Smith's views on foreign trade.)

Review Articles

710 "Adam Smith." *Outlook* 79 (January 2, 1905): 187–90. (Criticisms of Francis W. Hirsh's *Adam Smith.*)

711 Botha, D. J. J. "Adam Smith: A Homage from Germany." *South African Journal of Economics* 44 (December 1976): 412–16.

712 Checkland, Sydney G. "Adam Smith and the Biographer." *Scottish Journal of Political Economy* 14 (February 1967): 70–79. (Comments on John Rae's *Life of Adam Smith.*)

713 Gray, James. "Adam Smith Two Hundred Years Later: A Review

Article." *Dalhousie Review* 55, no. 3 (1975): 551–55.

714 Hutchison, Terrance W. "The Bicentenary of Adam Smith." *Economic Journal* 86 (September 1976): 481–92.

715 Scott, William R. "Books as Links of Empire: *The Wealth of Nations*." *Empire Review* (July 1923): 761–69.

716 Shenfield, Arthur. "A Wealth of Adam Smith." *Reason* 9, no. 7 (1977): 44–49.

717 [Tang, Anthony M.] "Discussion [of Naya's, Campbell's and Landes' Papers]." *American Economic Review* 57 (May 1967): 591–96. (Only Campbell's paper deals with Smith.)

718 Taylor, Overton H. "Frank Knight's Perspective 'On the History and Method of Economics.' " *Review of Economics and Statistics* 39 (August 1957): 342–45.

719 Unger, James A. "The Resurgence of Smithian Scholarship." *Polity* 12, no. 3 (1980): 491–508.

720 Viner, Jacob. "Possessive Individualism as Original Sin." *Canadian Journal of Economics and Political Science* 29 (November 1963): 559–66. (Brief references to Smith.)

721 White, Donald A. "Adam Smith's Wealth of Nations." *Journal of the History of Ideas* 37, no. 4 (1976): 715–20.

722 Wills, Gary. "Benevolent Adam Smith." *New York Review of Books* 25 (February 9, 1978): 40–43.

Selected Editions of Smith's Works

723 Smith, Adam. *The Early Writings of Adam Smith*, Edited by J. Ralph Lindgren. New York: Kelley, 1967. (Contents: Preface to William Hamilton's *Poems on Several Occasions*, 1748; articles in the *Edinburgh Review* of 1755; *Essays on Philosophical Subjects*, pp. 29–223, 1795; *Considerations Concerning the First Formation of Language*, 1761.)

724 Smith, Adam. *Essays on Philosophical Studies, with an Account of the Life and Writings of the Author*. Edited and with an introduction by Dugald Stewart. London: Cadell, 1759. Reprint ed., *The Early Writings of Adam Smith*, edited by J. R. Lindgren. New York: Kelley, 1967.

725 Smith, Adam. *An Inquiry into the Nature and Causes of the Wealth of Nations*. 2 vols. London: Printed for W. Strahan and T. Cadell, 1776.

726 Smith, Adam. *An Inquiry into the Nature and Causes of the Wealth*

of Nations. 3d ed., 3 vols., with additions. London: Printed for W. Strahan and T. Cadell, 1784. (This third edition served as the template for the Glasgow edition of *The Wealth of Nations.*)

727 Smith, Adam. *An Inquiry into the Nature and Causes of the Wealth of Nations,* 4 vols. With a life of the author, an introductory discourse, notes, and supplemental dissertations by J. R. McCulloch. Edinburgh: Black & Tait, 1828.

728 Smith, Adam. *An Inquiry into the Nature and Causes of the Wealth of Nations,* 2 vols. Edited, with an introduction, notes, marginal and summary, and an enlarged index by Edwin Cannan. New York: Putnam, 1904.

729 Smith, Adam. *An Inquiry into the Nature and Causes of the Wealth of Nations,* 2 vols. With an introduction by Professor Edwin R. A. Seligman. London: Dent, 1914.

730 Smith, Adam. *An Inquiry into the Nature and Causes of the Wealth of Nations.* With an introduction by Max Lerner. New York: Modern Library, 1937. (Reprint of the 1904 Cannan edition, with a lengthy introduction by the editor.)

731 Smith, Adam. *Lectures on Justice, Police, Revenue, and Arms: Delivered in the University of Glasgow by Adam Smith, Reported by a Student in 1763.* Edited and with an introduction and notes by Edwin Cannan. Oxford: Clarendon Press, 1896. Reprint ed., New York: Kelley, 1965.

732 Smith, Adam. *Lectures on Rhetoric and Belles Lettres: Delivered at the University of Glasgow by Adam Smith, Reported by a Student in 1762–63.* Edited with an introduction and notes by John M. Lothian. New York and London: T. Nelson, 1963.

733 Smith, Adam. *The Theory of Moral Sentiments.* London: Printed for A. Millar, 1759.

734 Smith, Adam. *The Theory of Moral Sentiments.* 6th ed. With considerable additions and corrections. London: Strahan & Cadell; Edinburgh: W. Creech & J. Bell, 1790.

735 Smith, Adam. *Works: with an Account of His Life and Writings by Dugald Stewart.* 5 vols. London: Cadell, 1811–12.

The Glasgow Editions

The following section gives the publications in the University of Glasgow's new edition of the works and correspondence of Adam Smith. The volumes in the edition meet the highest standards of scholarship and may be regarded as the definitive edition at the present time.

736 Smith, Adam. *The Glasgow Edition of the Works and Correspondence of Adam Smith.* 6 vols. Oxford: Clarendon Press, 1976–79. ("Commissioned by the University of Glasgow to celebrate the bicentenary of the *Wealth of Nations.*")
Vol. 1 *The Theory of Moral Sentiments*
Vol. 2 *An Inquiry into the Nature and Causes of the Wealth of Nations*
Vol. 3 *Essays on Philosophical Subjects*
Vol. 4 *Lectures on Rhetoric and Belles Lettres*
Vol. 5 *Lectures on Jurisprudence*
Vol. 6 *The Correspondence of Adam Smith*

737 Smith, Adam. *The Theory of Moral Sentiments.* The Glasgow Edition of the Works and Correspondence of Adam Smith, vol. 1. Edited by D. D. Raphael and A. L. Macfie. Oxford: Clarendon Press, 1976. ("The first scholarly edition in English . . . that systematically notes and analyzes all variations through the sixth edition.")

738 Smith, Adam. *An Inquiry into the Nature and Causes of the Wealth of Nations.* 2 vols. The Glasgow Edition of the Works and Correspondence of Adam Smith, vol. 2. General editors, R. H. Campbell and A. S. Skinner; textual editor, W. B. Todd. Oxford: Clarendon Press, 1976. ("The text printed here is that of the third edition of 1784." Introduction, 60 pp.; cross-references to Smith's other works and his sources; several appendixes.)

739 Smith, Adam. *Essays on Philosophical Subjects.* The Glasgow Edition of the Works and Correspondence of Adam Smith, vol. 3. Edited by D. D. Raphael and A. S. Skinner. Oxford: Clarendon Press, 1979.

740 Smith, Adam. *Lectures on Rhetoric and Belles Lettres.* The Glasgow Edition of the Works and Correspondence of Adam Smith, vol. 4. Edited by J. C. Bryce. Oxford: Clarendon Press, 1983.

741 Smith, Adam. *Lectures on Jurisprudence.* The Glasgow Edition of the Works and Correspondence of Adam Smith, vol. 5. Edited by R. L. Meek, D. D. Raphael, and P. G. Stein. Oxford: Clarendon Press, 1978. (An introduction; information on authentications and collation; many indexes.)

742 Smith, Adam. *The Correspondence of Adam Smith.* The Glasgow Edition of the Works and Correspondence of Adam Smith, vol. 6. Edited by Ernest Campbell Mossner and Ian Simpson Ross. Oxford: Clarendon Press, 1977. (The first complete edition of Smith's correspondence; letters are edited, annotated, and arranged chronologically.)

Author Index

Adam Smith Club, Glasgow, 636
Adam Smith Club, London, 637
Adelman, Irma, 326
Adiseshiah, Malcolm S., 390
Alchian, A., 638
Amano, Keitaro, 008
Angus-Butterworth, Lionel M., 117
Anikin, Andreĭ, 118
Anspach, Ralph, 308, 430
Archard, T., 022
Arrowood, Charles F., 464
Ashley, William, 335
Avila, Manuel, 309
Ayres, Clarence E., 565

Bagehot, Walter, 044, 085, 119
Bagolini, Luigi, 465
Baird, Robert M., 174
Barber, William J., 684
Barkai, Haim, 310
Bastable, Charles F., 566
Baudet, H., 609
Baumol, William J., 412, 543
Becker, James F., 497, 519
Bell, John F., 040, 253
Benians, Ernest A., 596
Bentham, Jeremy, 023
Berry, Christopher J., 610
Bevilacqua, Vincent, 611, 612
Billet, Leonard, 431, 552, 567
Bitterman, Henry J., 554, 555
Black, R. D. Collison, 119, 207
Bladen, Vincent W., 254, 273, 274, 288
Blanqui, Jérôme A., 255
Blaug, Mark, 275, 423, 639
Bloomfield, Arthur I., 344
Bodkin, Ronald G., 613
Bogardus, Emory, 685
Bonar, James, 001, 002, 009, 010, 086, 121, 345, 432, 466, 640
Bordo, M. D., 003
Botha, D. J. J., 711
Boulding, Kenneth E., 087, 224, 225

Bourne, Edward G., 168
Bowley, Marian, 256, 327
Bowman, Richard, 011
Bradley, Ian, 662
Branson, Roy, 433
Brenner, R., 311
Bronowski, Jacob, 076
Brown, A. H., 077, 078
Brown, E. H. Phelps, 373
Bryce, J. C., 614
Bryson, Gladys, 498, 686
Buchanan, David, 024
Buchanan, James M., 434, 467, 582
Buckle, Henry T., 562
Bullock, Charles, 014
Bullock, Charles J., 426, 428
Burt, Everett J., Jr., 257
Burton, John H., 025
Butler, R. J., 211

Cain, Roy E., 468
Cairncross, Alexander, 413
Camic, Charles, 499
Campbell, Roy H., 122
Campbell, Thomas, 123, 469, 470, 544, 568
Campbell, William F., 435, 471
Cannan, Edwin, 088, 169, 258, 289, 394, 583
Canterbery, E. Ray, 687
Carlyle, Alexander, 026
Carpenter, Kenneth E., 012
Catherwood, Benjamin F., 259
Chalk, Alfred F., 668
Chamley, P. E., 059
Chaudhuri, Asoke K., 312, 328, 336
Checkland, Sydney G., 364, 436, 712
Christensen, Paul P., 234
Clark, Andrew, 041
Clark, John M., 260, 604
Coase, Ronald H., 065, 437
Coats, Alfred W., 235, 414, 500, 520, 556
Cole, Arthur, 615
Colletti, Lucio, 472

Connolly, John M., 521
Cooke, C. A., 569
Cordasco, Francesco, 013
Cotterill, Charles F., 290
Cropsey, Joseph, 473, 474, 475
Cullison, W. E., 313
Cumming, Robert D., 501
Cunningham, William, 212, 346, 641

Danford, John W., 522
Dankert, Clyde E., 089, 124, 170, 171
Danner, Peter L., 438, 509
Das Gupta, A. K., 276, 277
Davenport, Herbert, 545
Davis, Joseph A., 617
Deane, Phyllis, 163
De Grood, David H., 546, 670
De Quincey, Thomas, 236, 237, 238
Desnitsky, S. E., 078
Devine, Donald J., 570
De Wilson, F. A. B., 261
Diamond, Sigmund, 172
Dickinson, H. T., 066
Dickinson, Z. Clark, 173
Dobb, Maurice H., 262, 291
Douglas, Paul H., 278, 292
Douglas, Roy, 347
Dow, Louis A., 618
Draper, William, 045
Dumont, Louis, 688
Duncan, Elmer H., 174
Dunn, William C., 439

Eagly, Robert V., 337
Earle, Edward M., 348
Ekelund, R. B., 125
Eliot, Thomas D., 571
Elliott, A. R. D., 042
Elliott, John E., 090, 229
Ellwood, C. A., 510
Eltis, Walter A., 329

Fagerstrom, Dalphy I., 597
Fanfani, Amitori, 127
Farrer, James A., 476
Fay, Charles R., 046, 091, 208, 338, 598, 663
Feingold, Richard, 642
Ferguson, Adam, 175

Fiering, Norman S., 440
Fischer, Norman, 536
Fleming, J. Marcus, 349
Flew, Anthony, 441
Flubacher, Joseph F., 689
Foley, Vernard, 376, 442, 511
Forbes, Duncan, 572, 584
Frankel, S. Herbert, 415
Franklin, Burt, 013
Franklin, Raymond S., 092
Freeman, R. D., 573
Friedman, Milton, 416, 417, 690
Friedson, E., 377
Fulton, R. B., 047

Galbraith, John K., 128, 671, 691
Gay, David E. R., 574
Gee, J. M., 213, 240
Gerber, J. C., 176
Gherity, James A., 177
Ghiselin, Michael T., 692
Ghosh, R. N., 605
Gide, Charles C., 129
Gill, Emily R., 443
Ginsberg, Eli, 130, 131, 374
Glenn, Gary D., 575
Golden, Soma, 093
Goss, Barry A., 444
Gottfried, P., 067
Graham, Malcolm K., 132
Gram, Harvey, 302
Gramm, Warren S., 523
Grampp, William D., 400, 445, 576, 599, 693
Grandjean, Burke D., 619
Gray, Alexander, 094
Gray, James, 713
Gray, John, 027
Gray, Simon, 028
Grigg, David, 620
Groenwegen, P. D., 178, 214, 378
Grossman, H., 672
Gruchy, Allan, 694
Guttridge, G. H., 179

Haakonssen, Knud, 585
Haggarty, John, 133
Haldane, Richard B., 048
Hamoway, Ronald, 379, 446

Haney, Lewis H., 263
Harrison, Frederick, 264
Harsanyi, John C., 446
Hartwell, R. N., 330
Harvard University Graduate School of Business Administration, Baker Library, 014
Hasbach, Wilhelm, 577
Hasek, Carl W., 226, 227
Hartwell, R. N., 330
Heckscher, Eli F., 350
Heilbroner, Robert L., 095, 537, 547, 621, 643, 673
Heimann, Eduard, 293
Heinrich, B., 524
Henderson, John P., 068, 241
Henry, J. F., 368
Hetzel, Robert L., 079
Hirschman, Albert O., 134
Hirst, Francis W., 049, 351
Hla Myint, U., 279, 294, 339
Hoar, W. P., 420
Hollander, Jacob H., 080, 081, 096, 180, 361
Hollander, Samuel, 097, 164, 181, 242, 265, 295, 314, 401
Holtrop, M. W., 674
Honour, Frances M., 695
Horne, George, 029
Horton, Samuel D., 365
Hoshino, Akio, 243
Howard, Michael, 662
Howell, Wilbur S., 644, 645
Hume, David, 030, 646
Hutchison, Terrance W., 098, 165, 714

Ingram, John K., 266

Jack, Henry H., 477
Jackson, J., 675, 676
Jadlow, J. M., 362
Jaffé, William, 099
Jensen, Hans E., 100, 677
Joerson, S. A., 031
Johnson, Harry G., 069, 418
Jones, Claude, 004
Jones, Reginald, 182
Jones, Robert A., 502
Joyce, Jeremiah, 032

Kaufman, M., 215
Kaushil, S., 280
Kay, John, 050
Khan, Mohammed, 315
Kilborn, Peter B., 622
Kindleberger, Charles P., 424
Kirk, Russell, 183
Kittrell, Edward, 402, 600
Knight, Frank H., 403, 696
Kobayashi, Noboru, 228
Koebner, Richard, 421, 606
Kurz, Heinz D., 244

Labini-Sylos, P., 296
Lackman, Conway L., 623
Laidler, D., 363
Laird, John, 548
Lamb, Robert B., 380, 503
La Nauze, John A., 184, 340
Land, Stephen K., 624
Landau, D., 003
Larmore, C., 448
Larsen, Robert M., 281, 282, 283, 297
Law, James T., 033
Leacock, Stephen, 101
Leake, Percy D., 267
Lee, Arthur, 034
Lee, Joseph, 625
Lekachman, Robert, 697
Lerner, Max, 136
Leslie, Thomas Edward Cliffe, 102, 601
Letiche, J. M., 331
Letwin, W., 103
Levy, David, 449, 626
Lewis, T. J., 369
Lewis, W. Arthur, 332
Lightwood, Martha B., 478
Lindgren, J. Ralph, 154, 512
Lockwood, William W., 316
Lowe, Adolph, 317, 333
Lowe, Robert, 082
Lundberg, I. C., 209
Lynn, Arthur D., Jr., 395

McCord, Norman, 352
McCosh, James, 479
McCulloch, John R., 051, 052, 053
MacDonald, Robert A., 245
Macfie, Alec, 186, 404, 450, 480, 557

McGarvey, C. J., 005
McGill, A. D., 451
MacLean, Kenneth, 452, 647
McNulty, Paul J., 284, 370, 381
MacPherson, Hector C., 137
Malek, James S., 627, 648
Malthus, Thomas R., 649
Mann, Fritz, K., 104
Marriott, J. A. R., 105
Marx, Karl, 698
Matthews, C. O., 397
Mayer, Joseph, 504
Mazlish, Bruce, 076
Meek, Ronald L., 187, 216, 229, 230, 285, 298, 355, 358, 382, 391
Merkel, Edward T., 060
Merrill, B., 525
Meyers, Milton L., 155, 246
Middendorf, John H., 188
Miller, S., 526
Miller, William L., 247, 311, 628
Mirowski, P. E., 217
Mitchell, A. A., 341
Mitchell, Wesley C., 138
Mizuti, Hiroshi, 014, 015, 481
Moos, S., 248, 678
Morgan, Frank, 650
Morrow, Glenn R., 268, 453, 454, 455, 482, 563
Moss, Laurence S., 106
Mossner, Ernest C., 054
Muir, Ethel, 483
Mumy, Gene E., 405
Murchison, Claudius, 107
Murray, David, 016
Musgrave, Richard A., 398
Myers, Milton M., 383
Myint, Hla. *See* Hla Myint, U.

Naggar, Tahaney, 406
Napoleoni, Claudio, 665
Neimanis, George J., 427
Nelson, John O., 189
Nicholson, Joseph S., 139, 218, 353, 396, 602
Nord, Walter, 527
Norton, D. F., 190

O'Brien, Denis P., 156
O'Connor, John, 679
Oncken, August, 558
Oser, Jacob, 140

Palyi, Melchior, 231
Papola, T. S., 249
Parrish, William J., 108
Patten, Simon N., 513, 699
Paul, Ellen F., 109, 484
Peacock, Alan T., 399
Petrella, Frank, 342, 549
Phillips, J. D., 629
Pike, Edgar R., 141, 651
Plenty, Arthur J., 110
Pokorný Dŭsan, 157
Political Economy Club, 666
Poor, Henry V., 366
Powers, Richard H., 528
Pownall, Thomas, 035
Price, Langford L., 070, 083, 392
Prior, Elizabeth, 456
Purves, George. *See* Gray, Simon
Putnam, Oliver, 142

Radner, John B., 457
Rae, John, 055, 191, 354
Ramsay, John, 232
Ranadive, K. R., 356
Randall, John H., 700
Raphael, David D., 061, 192, 485, 486, 487, 586
Rashid, S., 408
Rechtenwald, Horst C., 006, 233
Rees, Albert, 375
Reisman, David A., 538, 587
Ricardo, David, 701
Richardson, George B., 299
Rima, Ingrid H., 084
Rimlinger, Gaston V., 550
Rist, Charles, 129
Robbins, Caroline, 488
Robbins, Lionel, 300, 539, 702
Robertson, E. S., 043
Robertson, Hector M., 143, 286, 318
Robinson, Joan, 703
Rogers, James E. T., 193

Rogin, Leo, 269
Rohrlich, George F., 551
Roll, Eric, 111, 144
Romanos, John H., 630
Rosenberg, Nathan, 319, 357, 359, 384, 385, 529
Ross, Ian S., 194, 544
Rothschild, Lincoln, 631
Russell, Phillips, 704

Salomen, Albert, 505
Samuels, Warren J., 112, 113, 530, 531, 532, 533, 705
Samuelson, Paul A., 250, 680
Schneider, George E., 301
Schneider, Herbert L., 489
Schneider, Louis, 490
Schumpeter, Joseph, 158, 706
Schweber, Silvan S., 070, 072
Scott, William R., 017, 056, 062, 063, 145, 195, 196, 197, 198, 199, 458, 564, 652, 715
Selby-Bigge, Louis, 491
Shenfield, Arthur, 716
Shott, Susan S., 459
Sidgwick, Henry, 200
Simpson, David, 251
Singh, V. B., 320
Skinner, Andrew, 073, 159, 201, 202, 382, 460, 492, 514, 534, 540, 588, 589, 603, 666
Small, Albion W., 515
Smith, Adam, 036, 037, 210, 723, 724, 725, 726, 727, 728, 729, 730, 731, 732, 733, 734, 735, 736, 737, 738, 739, 740, 741, 742
Smith, Robert S., 203, 220
Sobel, Irvin, 535, 541
Soranzo, J. S., 578
Sowell, Thomas, 493, 542, 681
Spengler, Joseph J., 270, 321, 322, 323, 419, 516, 579
Spiegel, Henry W., 271, 506
Staley, Charles E., 343, 428
Stein, Peter G., 559
Stevens, David, 607
Stewart, Dugald, 057, 146

Stewart-Robertson, J. C., 190
Stigler, George J., 114, 386, 409, 580, 590, 707
Strong, Gordon, 517, 518
Sturges, R. P., 018
Swabey, William C., 494
Swengelwood, Alan, 507

Tame, Chris R., 252
Tang, Anthony M., 717
Taylor, N. W., 074
Taylor, Overton H., 166, 276, 461, 718
Taylor, William L., 064, 221, 286
Teichgraeber, R., 560
Temperley, Howard, 372
Thompson, Herbert F., 160
Thweatt, William L., 287, 324
Trivoli, George W., 653
Tronto, Joan C., 591
Tsanoff, Radoslav A., 495
Tucker, G. S. L., 360
Tufts, James H., 553

Unger, James, 592, 719

Van Den Haag, Ernest, 682
Vanderblue, Homer B., 019, 205
Veblen, Thorstein, 222, 223
Venning, Corey, 561
Vickers, Douglas, 367
Viner, Jacob, 058, 115, 147, 148, 149, 683, 708, 709, 720

Walsh, Vivian, 302
Walton, Paul, 303
Waters, W. R., 656
Watson, J. Wreford, 632, 654
Weaver, J. J., 633
Webster, A. M., 194
Weiss, D. D., 387
West, Edward, 038
West, Edwin G., 007, 150, 151, 161, 388, 389, 393, 410, 411, 462, 463, 581
Whitaker, Albert, 304
White, Donald A., 721
Wightman, William P., 167

Williams, Philip L., 305
Willis, Kirk, 206
Wills, Gary, 722
Wilson, George W., 152
Wilson, Thomas, 496, 655, 667
Winch, Donald, 593, 608
Wisman, Jon D., 425, 633
Withers, Hartley, 153
Wolf, Edward N., 306
Worland, Stephen T., 508, 634

Wrigley, E. A., 422
Wykes, Alan, 075

Yanaihara, Tadao, 020
Young, Jeffry T., 307
Young, William, 039
Youngson, Alexander J., 594

Zurawicki, S., 162
Zweig, Konrad, 325

Title Index

"An Account of the Life and Writings of Adam Smith," 146

Adam Smith, 049, 122, 137, 150

"Adam Smith," 076, 094, 117, 121, 129, 138, 144, 153, 259, 269, 291, 366, 466, 473, 494, 564, 710

"Adam Smith . . ." 263

Adam Smith, A Bibliographical Checklist: An International Record of Critical Writings and Scholarship Relating to Smith and Smithian Theory, 1876–1950, 013

"Adam Smith: A Homage from Germany," 711

"Adam Smith: A Reappraisal," 109

"Adam Smith, Adam Ferguson, and the Division of Labour," 379

"Adam Smith, Alexander Hamilton, Friedrich List: The Economic Foundations of Military Power," 348

"Adam Smith, America, and the Doctrinal Defeat of the Mercantile System," 598

"Adam Smith: An Aspect of Modern Economics?" 073

"Adam Smith: An Economic Interpretation of History," 540

Adam Smith: An Oration, 145

"Adam Smith and Alienation: A Rejoinder," 161

"Adam Smith and Alienation: Wealth Increases, Men Decay?" 393

"Adam Smith and Asia," 316

"Adam Smith and Belles Lettres: An Attempt to Establish the Philosophical Basis and to Formulate the Central Tenets of His Belletristic Thought," 650

"Adam Smith and David Ricardo on Economic Growth," 331

"Adam Smith and Edmund Burke: Complementary Contemporaries," 439

"Adam Smith and Foreign Trade," 338

"Adam Smith and German Social Thought," 067

"Adam Smith and Glasgow, Accompanying the New Glasgow Edition of the *Wealth of Nations*," 609

"Adam Smith and His Contemporaries," 605

"Adam Smith and His Foreign Critics," 215

"Adam Smith and His Friends," 042

"Adam Smith and His Relations to Recent Economics," 070, 083

"Adam Smith and James Anderson," 180

"Adam Smith and James Boswell," 170

"Adam Smith and Jurisprudence," 569

"Adam Smith and Laissez-faire," 115, 147, 148, 149

Adam Smith and Modern Political Economy: Bicentennial Essays on "The Wealth of Nations," 658

Adam Smith and Modern Sociology: A Study in the Methodology of the Social Sciences, 515

"Adam Smith and Natural Liberty," 568

"Adam Smith and Our Modern Economy," 119

"Adam Smith and Pitt," 351

"Adam Smith and Political Philosophy," 474

"Adam Smith and Property Rights Analysis," 574

"Adam Smith and Rousseau's *Discourse on Inequality:* Inspiration or Provocation?" 462

"Adam Smith and Society's Decision-makers," 516

"Adam Smith and Some Philosophical Origins of Eighteenth-century Rhetorical Theory," 611

"Adam Smith and Some Problems of Today," 105

"Adam Smith and the American Economic Community: An Essay in Applied Economics," 603

"Adam Smith and the American Revolutionists," 599

"Adam Smith and the Bankers," 364

"Adam Smith and the Biographer," 712

"Adam Smith and the City of Glasgow," 652

"Adam Smith and the Classical Concept of Profit," 355

"Adam Smith and the Classical Theory of Profit," 358

"Adam Smith and the Colonial Disturbances," 607

"Adam Smith and the Commercial Republic," 526

"Adam Smith and the Contemporary Social Exchange Theory," 527

"Adam Smith and the Currents of History," 260

"Adam Smith and the Development of the Labour Theory," 298

"Adam Smith and the Division of Labour," 391

"Adam Smith and the Division of Labour: A Bicentenary Estimate," 378

"Adam Smith and the Dynamic State," 091

"Adam Smith and the Economic Man," 400

"Adam Smith and the Economy as a System of Power," 530, 531

Adam Smith and the Eighteenth Century Concept of Social Progress, 517

"Adam Smith and the Eighteenth Century Concept of Social Progress," 518

"Adam Smith and the End of a Vision," 134

"Adam Smith and the Glasgow Merchants," 195

"Adam Smith and the History of Ideas," 167

"Adam Smith and the Human Stomach," 617

"Adam Smith and the Industrial Revolution," 330, 421, 423

"Adam Smith and the 'Infection' of David Hume's Society," 192

"Adam Smith and the Mercantile System," 414

"Adam Smith and the Nakaz of Catherine II," 078

Adam Smith and the Omnipresent State, 594

"Adam Smith and the Problem of Justice in Capitalist Society," 570

Adam Smith and the Role of the State: A Paper Delivered in Kircaldy . . . , 588

Adam Smith and the Scotland of His Day, 046

"Adam Smith and the Self-interest Axiom," 401

"Adam Smith and the Specie-flow Doctrine," 337

"Adam Smith and the Spirit of '76," 604

"Adam Smith and the Status Theory of Money," 367

"Adam Smith and the Theory of International Trade," 344

"Adam Smith and the Viet Nam War," 428

"Adam Smith and the *Wealth of Nations*," 098

Adam Smith and the "Wealth of Nations": An Adventure in Book Collecting and a Bibliography, 019

Adam Smith and the "Wealth of Nations": 1776–1976, 659

"Adam Smith as a Monetary Economist," 363

"Adam Smith as a Person," 044, 085

"Adam Smith as an Economist," 088

"Adam Smith as an Institutional Economist," 224

"Adam Smith as Critic of Ideas," 155
"Adam Smith as Imperialist," 595
"Adam Smith as Management Theorist," 374
"Adam Smith as Sociologist," 505
Adam Smith as Student and Professor . . . , 056
"Adam Smith at Downing Street, 1776–77," 196
Adam Smith, Author of "An Inquiry into the Nature and Causes of the Wealth of Nations,"
    and Thomas Paine, Author of "The Decline and Fall of the English System of Finance. . . ."
    031
The Adam Smith Centennial [*to Commemorate the Hundredth Anniversary of the Publication*
    of the "Wealth of Nations"], 116, 635
The Adam Smith Club, Glasgow, 1868–97, 636
[*Adam Smith Club, London.*] *. . . Rules, By-laws, and Members,* 637
"Adam Smith, Clubman," 040
"Adam Smith, Consumer Tastes, and Economic Growth," 529
"Adam Smith, Education, and Laissez-faire," 573
"Adam Smith, Empiricism, and the Rate of Profit in Eighteenth Century England," 217
"Adam Smith, Equality, and the Wealth of Sympathy," 522
Adam Smith: Father of the Science of Economics, 141
"Adam Smith in Theory and Practice," 493
Adam Smith: Man of Letters and Economist, 124
"Adam Smith: Moral Philosopher and Political Economist," 478
"Adam Smith: Moralist and Philosopher," 453, 482
"The Adam Smith Nobody Knows," 673
"Adam Smith on Abstinence," 444
"Adam Smith on Competition and Increasing Returns," 299
"Adam Smith on Human Capital," 579
"Adam Smith on International Economics," 336
"Adam Smith on Population Growth and Economic Development," 321
"Adam Smith on Productive and Unproductive Labour: A Theory of Full Development," 273
"Adam Smith on Profits—Paradox Lost and Regained," 357, 359
"Adam Smith on Prohibitory Duties, Text of a Letter to William Eden," 334
"Adam Smith on Public Debts," 396
"Adam Smith on Public Finance and Distribution," 398
"Adam Smith on the American Revolution: An Unpublished Memoir," 179
"Adam Smith on the Division of Labour: Two Views or One?," 384
"Adam Smith on the Need for Community Service: Quotations from *Wealth of Nations*," 625
"Adam Smith on Twentieth Century Finance," 394
"Adam Smith on Usury Laws," 362
"Adam Smith on Value," 276, 288
"Adam Smith on Wage Differentials Against Agricultural Laborers," 371
"Adam Smith on Wealth and Authority," 521
"Adam Smith: Philosophy and Science," 159
"Adam Smith, Practical Realist," 528
"Adam Smith Recognized Anew," 622
"Adam Smith Renaissance *Anno* 1776?" 006
"Adam Smith: Re-reading the Wealth of Nations," 103
"Adam Smith, Ricardo, and Economic Theory," 068
"Adam Smith: Science and the Role of the Imagination," 492

"Adam Smith, 1723 and 1923," 086

Adam Smith, 1723–1790, 476

"Adam Smith (1723–1790)," 125, 479

Adam Smith, 1776–1926 . . . , 660

"Adam Smith, 1776–1926," 096

Adam Smith, 1723–1973: Commemorative Symposium, 661

Adam Smith Speaks to Our Times: A Study of His Ethical Ideas, 047

Adam Smith: The Biographical Approach, 054

"Adam Smith: The Development of a System," 460

"Adam Smith: The Division of Labour," 392

"Adam Smith—The Heir and the Ancestor," 104

"Adam Smith: The Labor Market as the Basis of Natural Right," 369

Adam Smith: The Man and His Works, 151

"Adam Smith: The Modern Re-appraisal," 500

"Adam Smith: The Origin, Nature, and Function of Government," 589

Adam Smith . . . The Revolutionary Element in Adam Smith, 345

The Adam Smith Tradition . . . , 143

"Adam Smith Two Hundred Years Later: A Review Article," 713

"Adam Smith: Two Letters," 194

"Adam Smith, *Wealth of Nations,* and Edinburgh New Town," 654

"Adam Smith: What Kind of Institutionalist Was He?" 535

"Adam Smith's Analysis of the Imitative Arts and Instrumental Music," 648

"Adam Smith's Approach to the Theory of Value," 286

"Adam Smith's Commercial Society as a Surrogate for Morals," 525

"Adam Smith's Concept of Alienation," 380

"Adam Smith's Concept of Equilibrium," 246

"Adam Smith's Concept of Labor," 370

"Adam Smith's Conception of Self-interest in Economic and Political Affairs," 520

"Adam Smith's 'Considerations Concerning the First Formation of Languages,'" 624

"Adam Smith's 'Considerations' on Language," 610

"Adam Smith's Contribution to Eighteenth-century British Aesthetics," 627

"Adam Smith's Cost of Production Theory," 289

Adam Smith's Doctrine and the Present-day Crisis, 127

"Adam Smith's Economics of Politics," 410

"Adam Smith's Economics Revived in Election Year," 093

"Adam Smith's Empiricism and the Law of Nature, I," 554

"Adam Smith's Empiricism and the Law of Nature, II," 555

"Adam Smith's First Russian Disciple," 074

"Adam Smith's First Russian Followers," 077

"Adam Smith's Fiscal Ideas: An Eclectic Revisited," 395

"Adam Smith's Heavenly City," 506

"Adam Smith's Ideal and Theory of the Self-adjusting Liberal Economy," 272

Adam Smith's "Invisible Hand" in a Velvet Glove, 415

"Adam Smith's Jurisprudence: Between Morality and Economics," 559

"Adam Smith's Laissez-faire," 406

"Adam Smith's Lectures on Jurisprudence," 566

"Adam Smith's Lectures on Justice, Police, Revenue, and Arms," 577

"Adam Smith's 'Lectures on Rhetoric': An Historical Assessment," 644

"Adam Smith's Lectures on Rhetoric and Belles Lettres," 612

Adam Smith's Library: A Supplement to Bonar's Catalogue, with a Checklist of the Whole Library, 015
"Adam Smith's Library—Some Additions [to Bonar's Catalogue]," 004
Adam Smith's Moral and Political Philosophy, 489
"Adam Smith's *Moral Sentiments* as Foundation for His *Wealth of Nations,*" 557
"Adam Smith's 'Natural Law' and Contractual Society," 449
"Adam Smith's Philosophy of Riches," 463
"Adam Smith's Philosophy of Science," 160
"Adam Smith's Philosophy of Science and Theory of Social Psychology and Ethics," 166
"Adam Smith's Philosophy, Science, and Social Science," 485
Adam Smith's Politics: An Essay in Historiographic Revision, 593
"Adam Smith's Project of an Empire," 596
"Adam Smith's Public Economics," 581
"Adam Smith's Rejection of Hume's Price-Specie-Flow Mechanism: A Minor Mystery Resolved," 342
"Adam Smith's Relevance for 1976," 416, 417
Adam Smith's Science of Morals, 469
"Adam Smith's Shot Heard Round the World," 681
"Adam Smith's Social Welfare Function," 240
Adam Smith's Sociological Economics, 538
Adam Smith's Solicitude for the Poor and Skepticism About the Wealthy, 541
"Adam Smith's Status at Oxford," 041
"Adam Smith's System of Equilibrium Growth," 333
"Adam Smith's System: Sympathy not Self-interest," 503
"Adam Smith's Theory of Economic Development," 320
"Adam Smith's Theory of Economic Development (in Relation to Underdeveloped Economies)," 315
"Adam Smith's Theory of Economic Growth," 329
"Adam Smith's Theory of Economic Growth, Part I," 322
"Adam Smith's Theory of Economic Growth, Part II," 323
"Adam Smith's Theory of Inquiry," 154
"Adam Smith's Theory of International Trade in the Perspective of Economic Development," 339
"Adam Smith's Theory of Justice, Prudence, and Beneficence," 435
"Adam Smith's Theory of Market Prices," 281
"Adam Smith's *Theory of Moral Sentiments,*" 450
"Adam Smith's Theory of Production and Distribution," 282
"Adam Smith's Theory of Social Science," 497
"Adam Smith's Theory of Value and Distribution," 278, 297
"Adam Smith's Two Views on the Division of Labour," 388
"Adam Smith's View of Man," 437
"Adam Smith's Views on National Defence," 426, 429
"Adam Smith's Wealth of Nations," 721
[Addenda to] "A Catalogue of the Library of Adam Smith," 001, 002
"After Samuelson, Who Needs Adam Smith?" 087
"Against the New Mercantilism: The Relevance of Adam Smith," 252
The Age of Uncertainty, 691
"Agrarian Economists: The Physiocrats and Adam Smith," 647
"Alexander Hamilton and Adam Smith," 168

All Classes Productive of National Wealth; or, The Theories of M. Quesnai, Dr. Adam Smith and Mr. Gray . . . , 028

Analysis of Adam Smith's "Wealth of Nations," 261

"Another Advantage of the Division of Labor," 385

"The Art of Sympathy in Eighteenth-century British Moral Thought," 457

"The Ascendancy of Society: Adam Smith and the Apolitical Vision of the Augustan Age," 592

"The Author of the *Wealth of Nations*," 043

Back to Adam Smith, 641

"Benevolent Adam Smith," 722

"Beyond Adam Smith's Economics," 235

A Bibliographic List of Essays on the Economic Theory of Adam Smith, 011

"The Bicentenary of Adam Smith," 714

Biographical Memoir of Adam Smith, LL.D., of William Robertson, D.D. and Thomas Reid, D.D., 057

"Books as Links of Empire, *The Wealth of Nations*," 715

British Moralists, 491

"Bucolic Tradition and Virtuous Work: Arthur Young and Adam Smith," 642

"Bunker Hill, Tory Propaganda, and Adam Smith," 172

"Burdens of Monopoly: Classical Versus Neoclassical," 411

Burke and Adam Smith, 208

Capital: Adam Smith, Karl Marx, 267

"Capitalism, Slavery, and Ideology," 372

"The Case of Adam Smith's Value Analysis," 280

A Catalogue of the Library of Adam Smith, Author of the "Moral Sentiments" and "The Wealth of Nations," 009, 010

"A Centenarian on a Bicentenarian: Leon Walras's Elements of Adam Smith's *Wealth of Nations*," 099

Classical and Marxian Political Economy: Essays in Honor of Ronald L. Meek, 662

Classical and Neoclassical Theories of General Equilibrium: Historical Origins and Mathematical Structure, 302

"Classical Economics and Its Moral Critics," 445

Classical Economics Reconsidered, 542

Classical Political Economy and the Colonies, 608

"The Classical School: Adam Smith," 140

Classical Theories of Value: From Smith to Sraffa, 307

"The Classical Theory of Economic Growth," 317

The Classical Theory of Economic Policy, 705

"The Classical Theory of Economic Policy: Non-legal Social Controls, Part I," 532

"The Classical Theory of Economic Policy": Non-legal Social Controls, Part II," 533

"Command over Labour: A Study in Misrepresentation," 274

"The Commemoration of Adam Smith at Glasgow," 669

"[Communication Relating to the Muir Portrait of Adam Smith]", 630

"Compensating Wage Differentials," 375

"Competition: The Product Markets," 296

A Complete Analysis or Abridgement of Dr. Adam Smith's "Inquiry into the Nature and Causes of the Wealth of Nations," 032
The Concept of Ethics in the History of Economics, 689
"The Conflict Between Montesquieu and Hume: A Study of the Origins of Adam Smith's Universalism," 059
"A Conjecture About Adam Smith," 182
"The Consistency of Adam Smith," 558
A Contribution to the Critique of Political Economy, 698
"[Conversation Between] Adam Smith and Highland Laird," 616
Corn Trade, An Examination of Certain Commercial Principles . . . as Laid Down in the Fourth Book of Mr. Adam Smith's Treatise on the "Wealth of Nations," 039
"The Corporation Spirit and Its Liberal Analysis," 519
The Correspondence of Adam Smith, 742

"Darwin and the Political Economists: Divergence of Character," 071
"David Easton and the Invisible Hand," 578
"David Hume and Adam Smith: A Study in Intellectual Kinship," 468
"The Dawn of a Science," 080
Defense of Usury . . . To Which Is Added a Letter to Adam Smith . . . , 023
"The Development of Adam Smith's Ideas on the Division of Labour," 382
Development of Economic Analysis, 084
The Development of English Thought: A Study in the Economic Interpretation of History, 513
"The Development of the Theory of Colonization in English Classical Political Economy," 600
"The Development of the Theory of Money from Adam Smith to David Ricardo," 361
"A Diagrammatic Presentation of Adam Smith's Growth Model," 324
Dialogue in Political Economy: Translations from and into German in the 18th Century, 012
"The Diffusion of Development," 332
"[Discussion of] Naya's, Campbell's, and Landes' Papers," 717
"Division of Labour as a Principle of Social Cohesion," 383
"Division of Labor as Social Interaction," 377
"The Division of Labor in Plato and Smith," 376
"The Division of Labor Is Limited by the Extent of the Market," 386
"The Division of Labor, Technology, and Education: Cross-national Evidence," 619
"Dmitriev's Smithian Model," 283
"Dr. Johnson and Adam Smith," 188

"Early Formulators of Say's Law," 287
Early Writings of Adam Smith, 723
Economic Liberalism, 693
Economic Philosophy, 703
"The Economics and Economic Theories of Adam Smith: A Study of Social Conceptions in the Eighteenth Century," 268
"Economics and History," 201
"Economics and the Idea of Ius Naturale," 461
"Economics as Physics—Adam Smith," 293
"Economics as Social Economics: The Views of the 'Founding Fathers,' " 677
The Economics of Adam Smith, 265
"The Economics of Adam Smith: Professor Hollander's Reappraisal," 106
"The Economics of Education in English Classical Political Economy: A Re-examination," 639

"The Economics of Imperialism," 602

"Economists and the History of Ideas," 680

Economists' Papers 1750–1950: A Guide to Archive and Other Manuscript Sources for the History of British and Irish Economic Thought, 018

Economy and Self: Philosophy and Economics from the Mercantilists to Marx, 536

The Economy of Nature and the Evolution of Sex, 692

"Editor's Introduction: History of the Report: Value of the Report . . ." 583

Eighteenth-century British Logic and Rhetoric, 645

"Eighteenth Century Scottish Political Economy: The Impact on Adam Smith and His Work of His Association with Francis Hutcheson and David Hume," 221

The Emergence of the Theory of the Firm: From Adam Smith to Alfred Marshall, 305

"Emerson and the Political Economists," 176

Empire, 606

"Enter an Economist," 704

An Essay in Vindication of the Continental Colonies of America, from a Censure of Mr. Adam Smith . . . , 034

Essays in Economic Theory, 699

Essays in Economic Thought, Aristotle to Marshall, 270

Essays on Adam Smith, 667

Essays on Philosophical Studies . . . , 724, 739

The Essential Principles of the Wealth of Nations, Illustrated, in Opposition to Some False Doctrines of Dr. Adam Smith and Others, 027

The Ethical and Economic Theories of Adam Smith, 563

The Ethical System of Adam Smith, 483

"The Ethics of Sympathy," 495

"The Ethics of the *Wealth of Nations,*" 454, 545

"Euge! Belle! Dear Mr. Smith: *The Wealth of Nations,* 1776–1976," 318

The Evolution of Economic Ideas, 163

Evolutionary Economics, 225

"The Evolutionist Revolt Against Classical Economics," 672

An Examination of the Doctrines of Value, as Set Forth by Adam Smith, Ricardo, McCulloch, Mill, etc., 290

"Examining the Effect of Interdependent Consumer Preferences on Economic Growth, or, Rediscovering Adam Smith and His Eighteenth Century Contemporaries," 313

"The First Spanish Edition of the *Wealth of Nations,*" 203

"A Formal Outline of a Smithian Growth Model," 310

"The Founder of a School," 081

"The Founding Faith: Adam Smith's *Wealth of Nations,*" 128

Four Autographed Letters of Adam Smith to Lord Hailes, 210

"Francis Hutcheson and Adam Smith," 488

Francis Hutcheson and David Hume as Predecessors of Adam Smith, 064

Francis Hutcheson: His Life, Teaching, and Position in the History of Philosophy, 062

"Frank Knight's Perspective 'On the History and Method of Economics,'" 718

Free Trade: Theory and Practice from Adam Smith to Keynes, 352

French Translations of the Wealth of Nations, 016

From Adam Smith to Maynard Keynes: The Heritage of Political Economy, 254

From Alienation to Surplus Value, 303

From Mandeville to Marx: The Genesis and Triumph of Economic Ideology, 688

A Full and Detailed Catalogue of Books Which Belonged to Adam Smith, Now in the

Possession of the Faculty of Economics, University of Tokyo, with Notes and Explanations, 020

"Further Technological Relationships in *The Wealth of Nations* and in Ricardo's *Principles,*" 251

"Further Thoughts on the Aesthetics of Adam Smith," 631

"Giving Back Words: Things, Money, Persons," 501
Glasgow Edition of the Works and Correspondence of Adam Smith, 736
Greek Influence on Adam Smith, 063
"Growth and Progress: The Nineteenth Century View in Britain," 436
The Growth of Economic Thought, 271
"Guide to John Rae's Life of Adam Smith," 058

"Haggis and the *Wealth of Nations,*" 682
"Has the Authorship of the 'Abstract' Really Been Decided?" 189
"Henry Home of Kames as Predecessor to Adam Smith," 060
"The Historical Background: Adam Smith and the Industrial Revolution," 424
"The Historical Dimension of the *Wealth of Nations,*" 164
History and Criticism of the Labor Theory of Value in English Political Economy, 304
"History and Political Economy: Smith, Marx, and Marshall," 214
History of Civilization in England, 562
A History of Economic Analysis, 706
A History of Economic Ideas, 697
A History of Economic Thought, 684
History of Political Economy in Europe, 255
A History of Theories of Production and Distribution in English Political Economy from 1776 to 1848, 258
"Homage to Adam Smith," 095
The House of Adam Smith, 130
"The House of Adam Smith," 131
Human Documents of Adam Smith's Time, 651
"Hume and Adam Smith," 702
"Hume and Adam Smith on Justice and Utility," 586

"Imagination and Sympathy: Sterne and Adam Smith," 452
"The Impartial Spectator," 487
The Impartial Spectator, 486
"The Implications of the *Theory of Moral Sentiments* for Adam Smith's Economic Thought," 430
"Inalienable Rights and Positive Government in the Modern World," 575
"The Inaugural Address: T and Sympathy," 211
"An Incident in the Life of Adam Smith, Commissioner of His Majesty's Customs," 205
"The Individual and the Creation of Social Forces—Adam Smith," 553
"The Individual and the State: Some Contemporary Problems," 418
"Individual, Group, or Government? Smith, Mill, and Sidgwick," 549
The Individual in Society: Papers on Adam Smith, 480
"Individualistic Social Thought," 685
"The Industrial Revolution and the Free Market," 420
An Inquiry into the Nature and Causes of the Wealth of Nations, 725, 726, 727, 728, 729, 730, 738
"An Inquiry into the Social Aspects of Adam Smith's Theory of Value," 509

The Intellectual History of Laissez-faire, 708

"The Intellectual History of Laissez-faire," 683

"The Introduction of Adam Smith on the Continent," 231

The Introduction of Adam Smith's Doctrines into Germany, 227

"The Introduction of Adam Smith's Doctrines into Germany," 226

[Introduction to] "An Inquiry into the Nature and Causes of the Wealth of Nations," by Adam Smith, 051

Introductory Essay on Adam Smith's "Wealth of Nations" . . . , 139

"The Invisible Hand," 690

"The Invisible Hand Loses Its Grip," 524

"The Invisible Hand of Jupiter," 186

"Irresistible Compassion: An Aspect of Eighteenth-century Sympathy and Humanitarianism," 440

"Is Adam Smith Out of Date?" 248

"Is It Consistent with the Design and Practice of Adam Smith to Treat the Laws of Industry as an Independent and Abstract Science?" 264

"Is Political Rationality Possible? A Critique of Political Control in the Work of Hobbes, Smith, and Weber," 591

"James Madison and the Scottish Enlightenment," 433

James Steuart, Adam Smith, and Friedrich List, 228

"Jefferson and the Scottish Enlightenment: A Critique of Gary Wills's Inventing America . . ." 446

"Jettisoning of Adam Smith," 110

"The Just Economy: The Moral Basis of the *Wealth of Nations,*" 431

"Justice in Adam Smith: The Right and the Good," 443

"Justice, Liberty, and Economy," 552

"The Justice of Natural Liberty," 434, 467

"The Labour Market," 373

"Laissez-faire in English Classical Economics," 402

"Laissez-faire, Planning, and Ethics," 678

"Laissez-faire, Pro and Con," 403

Land Reform in the British Isles and Adam Smith and Free Trade, 347

"Land Use and Adam Smith: A Bicentennial Note," 632

"The Language of Economists," 671

"Later Eighteenth-century British Social Philosophy," 510

Lectures on Jurisprudence, 741

Lectures on Justice, Police, Revenue, and Arms . . . , 731

Lectures on Rhetoric and Belle Lettres, 732, 740

"A Letter from Adam Smith," 173

Letter from Adam Smith, LL.D. to Mr. Strahan [upon] the Death of Hume, 036

A Letter from Governor Pownall to Adam Smith . . . Being an Examination of Several Points of Doctrine, Laid Down in His "Inquiry into the Nature and Causes of the Wealth of Nations," 035

"A Letter of Adam Smith to Henry Dundas, 1789," 185

"Letter of Adam Smith to the Duke of La Rochefoucauld," 191

"A Letter of Adam Smith [to William Pultney, M.P.]," 193

A Letter to Adam Smith, LL.D., on the Life, Death, and Philosophy of His Friend David Hume Esq., 029

A Letter to His Grace the Duke of Buccleugh on National Defence: With Some Remarks on Dr. Smith's Chapter on the Subject . . ., 026

A Letter to Sir William Pultney, in Consequence of His Proposal for Establishing a New Bank, 037

"Letter to the Editor on Smith's 'Relation Between Local and Imperial Taxation,'" 200

The Letters of David Hume, 646

Life and Correspondence of David Hume, 025

Life of Adam Smith, 048, 055

The Life of David Hume, Esq., 030

Life of Dr. Adam Smith, 045

"Literary Views of Adam Smith," 614

"The Longevity of Adam Smith's Vision: Paradigms, Research Programmes, and Falsifiability in the History of Economic Thought," 156

"The Macro and Micro Aspects of the *Wealth of Nations*," 241

The Making of Economics, 687

Man and Society: The Scottish Inquiry of the Eighteenth Century, 686

"Mandeville, Rousseau, and Smith," 472

"A Manuscript Attributed to Adam Smith," 184

"A Manuscript Criticism of *The Wealth of Nations* in 1776, by Hugh Blair," 197

"The Manuscript of Adam Smith's Glasgow Lectures," 198

"The Manuscript of an Early Draft of Part of *The Wealth of Nations*," 199'

"Marcuse, Metaphysics, and Marxism," 626

"The Market and the State," 413

The Market and the State: Essays in Honour of Adam Smith, 664

"Marx Versus Smith on the Division of Labor," 387

"Mechanistic Analogy and Smith on Exchange," 634

Mercantilism, 350

"Mercantilism and Free Trade Today," 349

"Militia Versus the Standing Army in the History of Economic Thought from Adam Smith to Friedrich Engels," 427

"Models of Production and Exchange in the Thought of Adam Smith and David Ricardo," 306

"The Modern Development of Classical Rent Theory," 623

Modern Economic Thought: The American Tradition, 694

"A Modern Theorist's Vindication of Adam Smith," 250

"Moral Judgment," 448

"The Moral Justification of Free Enterprise: A Lay Sermon on an Adam Smith Text," 404

"Moral Philosophy and Civil Society," 481

"The Moral Philosophy of Adam Smith," 477

Moral Revolution and Economic Science: The Demise of Laissez-faire in Nineteenth Century British Political Economy, 484

"Morality and the Theory of Rational Behavior," 447

Nassau Senior and Classical Economics, 256

"Nations of Wealth," 407

"Natural History in the Age of Adam Smith," 534

"Natural Law and the Rise of Economic Individualism in England," 668
"The New Era: 'Homo Oeconomicus,' " 546
"The New Era: The Rosy Dawn and Revolutionary Theory," 670
"New Light on Adam Smith," 458
"New Light on Adam Smith's Glasgow Lectures on Jurisprudence," 187
"A Note on Adam Smith's Second Regulator of Wealth," 675, 676
"A Note on Adam Smith's Version of the Vent for Surplus Model," 343
"A Note on the Division of Labor in Plato and Smith," 381
"A Note on the History of Perfect Competition," 284
"Notes on Adam Smith's Library and the Bonar Catalogue, 1932," 005

"Observations on Smith's *Wealth of Nations*," 142
Observations on the Subjects Treated in Dr. Smith's "Inquiry into the Nature and Cause [sic] of the Wealth of Nations," 024
"Of the Principle of Moral Estimation: A Discourse Between David Hume, Robert Clerk, and Adam Smith. An Unpublished Mss.," 175
"On Camic's Antipresentist Methodology," 502
"On Corporations: A Visit with Smith," 638
"On Professor Samuelson's Canonical Classical Model of Political Economy," 181
On Revolutions and Progress in Economic Knowledge, 165
"On the Definition and Application of Terms by Adam Smith," 649
On the History and Method of Economics: Selected Essays, 696
"On the Politics of the Classical Economists," 576
On the Principles of Political Economy and Taxation, 701
"On the *Wealth of Nations*," 089
"The Opinions of Ricardo and of Adam Smith on Some of the Leading Doctrines of Political Economy Stated and Compared," 219
"Origin of Rent in Adam Smith's Wealth of Nations: An Anti-neoclassical View," 213
"The Origin of the Origin Revisited," 072
"Origins of Capitalist Development: A Critique of Neo-Smithian Marxism," 311
"Origins of Sociology: The Case of the Scottish Enlightenment," 507

"The Paradox of Adam Smith," 136
"The Paradox of Progress: Decline and Decay in the *Wealth of Nations*," 621, 643
The Parity of Moneys as Regarded by Adam Smith, Ricardo, and Mill, 365
"The Part of Adam Smith on the Development of Economic Thought," 162
"Part 1. Adam Smith," 008
"The Pattern of Citations in Economic Theory, 1945–68: An Exploration Towards a Quantitative History of Thought," 003
"Perfect Competition Historically Contemplated," 409
"Perfect Man, Perfect Competition, and the Spoils of War," 504
"Philosophy, Welfare, and 'The System of Natural Liberty,' " 508
"Pitt as Chancellor of the Exchequer," 075
"Policy of Laissez-faire During Scarcities," 408
"Political Affairs," 556
Political Economy: A Historical Perspective, 233
Political Economy Club . . . Revised Report of the Proceedings . . . Held in Celebration of the Hundredth Year of the Publication of the "Wealth of Nations," 666
"The Political Economy of Adam Smith," 102, 112, 113

"The Political Economy of Adam Smith: Then and Now," 090
"The Political Economy of Alienation: Karl Marx and Adam Smith," 389
"Political Order and Economic Development: Reflections on Adam Smith's *Wealth of Nations*," 567
"The Politics of Edward Gibbon," 066
"The Politics of Political Economists," 707
Polity and Economy: An Interpretation of the Principles of Adam Smith, 475
The Poor Man's Garden . . . with a Reference to the Opinions of Dr. A. Smith in His "Wealth of Nations," 033
"Possessive Individualism as Original Sin," 720
"A Postscript," 277
"Preconceptions of Economic Science, I," 222
"Preconceptions of Economic Science, II," 223
Precursors of Adam Smith: Readings in Economic History and Theory, 230
Price of Corn and Wages of Labour, with Observations upon Dr. Smith's and Mr. Ricardo's Doctrines upon Those Subjects . . ., 038
"A 'Primitive' Equilibrium System: A Neglected Aspect of Smith's Economics," 249
"Primogeniture, Entails, and Endowments in English Classical Economics," 628
"The Process of Modernization and Industrial Revolution in England," 422
"Productive Labour, Exploitation, and Oppression—A Perspective," 368
"The Progress of Economic Doctrine in England in the Eighteenth Century," 212
A Project of Empire: A Critical Study of the Economics of Imperialism, with Special Reference to the Ideas of Adam Smith, 353
"Prudence, Justice, and Beneficence," 471
"Public Goods and Natural Liberty," 582
"Public Policy and Monetary Expenditure," 397
"Puzzles of the *Wealth of Nations*," 615

"A Quest for the Unrecognized Publication of Adam Smith," 177

"The Reaction in Favor of the Classical Political Economy," 218
Readings in the Development of Economic Analysis, 1776–1848, 120
"The Relations Between Adam Smith and Benjamin Franklin," 571
The Relevance of Adam Smith, 079
"The Relevance of *The Wealth of Nations* to Contemporary Economic Policy," 069
"Resource Allocation and the Beginnings of Welfare Economics in Adam Smith's Theory of Economic Policy," 301
"The Resurgence of Smithian Scholarship," 719
"Rethinking das Adam Smith Problem," 560
"A Retrospect of Free Trade Doctrine," 335, 341
"A Retrospective Look at Adam Smith's Views on University Education," 613
"Revising Adam Smith," 107
"Ricardo and Adam Smith," 262
"Ricardo Made Easy; or, What Is the Radical Difference Between Ricardo and Smith? . . . Part I," 236
"Ricardo Made Easy; or, What Is the Radical Difference Between Ricardo and Smith? Part II," 237
"Ricardo Made Easy; or, What Is the Radical Difference Between Ricardo and Smith? Part III," 238

"Ricardo's Criticisms of Adam Smith," 245
Richard Cobden and Adam Smith: Two Lectures, 346
"Richard Jones's Contribution to the Theory of Rent," 247
"The Rise of the City: Adam Smith Versus Henri Pirenne," 618
Robert Torrens and the Evolution of Classical Economics, 300
"The Role in Parliament of the Economic Ideas of Adam Smith, 1776–1800," 206
"The Role of Self-interest in the Social Economy of Life, Liberty and the Pursuit of Happiness, *Anno* 1976 and Beyond," 551
"The Role of Technology in Economic Thought: Adam Smith to John Maynard Keynes," 425
"The Role of Utility and Demand in *The Wealth of Nations,*" 295

"Science and Ideology," 158
A Science in Its Youth: Pre-Marxian Political Economy, 118
The Science of a Legislator: The Natural Jurisprudence of David Hume and Adam Smith, 585
"The Science of Man—The Sciences of Human Nature and of Business," 700
"Scientific Explanation and Ethical Justification in the *Moral Sentiments,*" 470
"Scientific Whiggism, Adam Smith, and John Millar," 572
Scotland and Scotsmen in the Eighteenth Century, 232
"Scotland's Resurgent Economist: A Survey of the New Literature on Adam Smith," 007
The Scottish Moralists on Human Nature and Society, 490
"Scottish Opinion and the American Revolution," 597
"The Selective Interpretation of Adam Smith," 523
A Series of Original Portraits and Caricature Etchings . . . with Biographical Sketches and Illustrative Anecdotes, 050
"The Significance of the Doctrine of Sympathy in Hume and Adam Smith," 455
"Sir James Steuart and Land Use Theory: A Note," 620
"Sir James Steuart: Author of a System," 202
"Skeptical Whiggism, Commerce, and Liberty," 584
Sketch of the Life and Writings of Adam Smith, L.L.D., 052, 053
"Smith, Adam," 135
"Smith, Adam (1723–90)," 126
"Smith and Marshall on the Individual's Supply of Labor: A Note," 679
"Smith and Ricardo: Aspects of the Nineteenth-century Legacy," 097
"Smith and the Greeks: A Reply to Professor McNulty's Comments," 442
"Smith and the Merits of the Poor," 550
"Smith and Undeveloped [*sic*] Nations," 309
"Smith and Walras: Two Theories of Science," 157
Smith, Marx, and After: Ten Essays in the Development of Economic Thought, 229
"Smith, Marx, and Malthus," 633
"Smith on 'Distributins,' " 456
Smith, Ricardo, Marx, 665
"Smith, Turgot, and the 'Four Stages' Theory," 216
"Smith Versus Hobbes: Economy Versus Polity," 419
"Smith Versus Marx on Business Morality and the Social Interest," 412, 543
"Smithian Economics and Its Pernicious Legacy," 092
"Smithian Themes in Piero Sraffa's Theory," 244
"Smith's Contribution in Historical Perspective," 207
"Smith's Growth Paradigm," 308
"Smith's Theory of Value and Distribution," 292

"Smith's Travels on the Ship of State," 580, 590

"Social and Institutional Dimensions of the Theory of Capitalism in Classical Political Economy," 239

"Social Economics of Adam Smith [symposium]," 656

Social Perspectives in the History of Economic Theory, 257

The Social Philosophy of Adam Smith, 512

"The Social Philosophy of Smith's *Wealth of Nations,*" 548

The Social Physics of Adam Smith, 511

"Socialization of the Individual in Adam Smith," 547

"Society, Self, and Mind in Moral Philosophy: The Scottish Moralists as Precursors of Symbolic Interactionism," 459

"Some Aspects of the Treatment of Capital in *The Wealth of Nations,*" 327

"Some Concluding Reflections," 655

"Some Eighteenth-century Conceptions of Society," 498

"Some Implications of Adam Smith's Analysis of Investment Priorities," 314

"Some Institutional Aspects of the *Wealth of the Nations,*" 319

"Some Technological Relationships in the *Wealth of Nations* and Ricardo's *Principles,*" 242

Some Thoughts on Adam Smith's Theory of the Division of Labour, 390

"Sources and Contours of Adam Smith's Conceptualized Reality in the *Wealth of Nations,*" 100

"Sraffian Themes in Adam Smith's Theory," 234

The State of the Industrial Revolution in 1776, 695

Statement of Some New Principles on the Subject of Political Economy, Exposing the Fallacies of the System of Free Trade and Some of the Other Doctrines Maintained in the "Wealth of Nations," 354

Studies in the Theory of International Trade, 709

"Studies Relating to Adam Smith During the Last Fifty Years," 017

"The Substance of Adam Smith's Attack on Mercantilism," 340

"The Successes and Failures of Professor Smith," 114

The Suffolk Bank, 653

Suppression of the French Nobility Vindicated, . . . to Which Is Added a Comparative View of Dr. Smith's System of the Wealth of Nations . . . , 022

"Sympathy and Exchangeable Value: Keys to Adam Smith's Social Philosophy," 438

"Sympathy and Self-interest," 496

The Synthetic "Wealth of Nations" . . . , 132

"A System of Power in Adam Smith's Theory," 243

A System of Social Science: Papers Relating to Adam Smith, 514

The Tables Turned, 640

Tawney, Galbraith, and Adam Smith: State and Welfare, 587

Theories of Economic Growth and Development, 326

"Theories of the Velocity of Circulation of Money in Earlier Economic Literature," 674

Theories of Welfare Economics, 294

"Theory and Experience in Adam Smith," 451

The Theory of Economic Policy in English Classical Political Economy, 539

Theory of Education in the Political Philosophy of Adam Smith, 464

The Theory of Moral Sentiments, 733, 734, 737

"The *Theory of Moral Sentiments* by Adam Smith, 1759," 432

"The Theory of Small Enterprise: Smith, Mill, Marshall, and Marx," 629

"The Theory of the Wise and Virtuous Man," 123
"Third Modern Phase: System of Natural Liberty," 266
"Thomas Reid on Adam Smith's Theory of Morals," 190
"Thomas Reid's Criticisms of Adam Smith's *Theory of Moral Sentiments*," 174
"Three Pillars of Order: Edmund Burke, Samuel Burke, Samuel Johnson, Adam Smith," 183
"Three Questions About Justice in the 'Treatise,' " 441
"The Topicality of Adam Smith's Notion of Sympathy and Judicial Evaluations," 465
"Town and Country in Adam Smith's *The Wealth of Nations*," 405
"The Transition: Adam Smith," 360
"The Treatment of the Principles of Public Finance in *The Wealth of Nations*," 399
" 'The True Old Humean Philosophy' and Its Influence on Adam Smith," 061
"Turgot and Adam Smith," 178
Turgot's Unknown Translator: The "Reflexions" and Adam Smith, 209
"Two Eighteenth Century Celebrities," 171
"Two Letters of Adam Smith's," 169

"An Unpublished Letter of Adam Smith," 204
"Utilitarianism of Adam Smith's Policy Advice," 544
"Utilitarians Revisited," 499

"Value in the History of Economic Thought," 285
The Vanderblue Memorial Collection of Smithiana: An Essay by J. Charles Bullock . . ., 014

"A Wealth of Adam Smith," 716
"The *Wealth of Nations*," 065, 253, 565
The "Wealth of Nations": An Analysis with Special Reference to Underdeveloped Countries, 328
"*The Wealth of Nations* and the Slave Trade," 601
"*The Wealth of Nations* and Underdeveloped Countries," 312
"*Wealth of Nations*: Bicentenary, a Symposium," 657
"The *Wealth of Nations*, by A. Smith," 152
"The *Wealth of Nations* in Spain and Hispanic America, 1780–1930," 220
"The *Wealth of Nations*, 1776–1976," 111
"*The Wealth of Nations*—The Vision and the Conceptualization," 356
"The 'Wealth of the Nations,' with Notes, Supplementary Chapters, and A Life of Dr. Smith," 021
"Welfare Indices in the *Wealth of Nations*," 275
"The Welfare Significance of Productive Labour," 279
"What Are the More Important Results Which Have Followed from the Publication of the *Wealth of Nations* . . .?" 082
"What Is Left of Adam Smith?" 101
The Wisdom of Adam Smith, 133
"With Due Respect to Adam Smith," 108
"The Wonderful World of Adam Smith," 537
Works, 735
The World of Adam Smith, 663
"The World of Adam Smith Revisited," 561

"Yesterday's Predictions: Smith, Malthus, Ricardo, and Mill: The Forerunners of Limits to Growth," 325